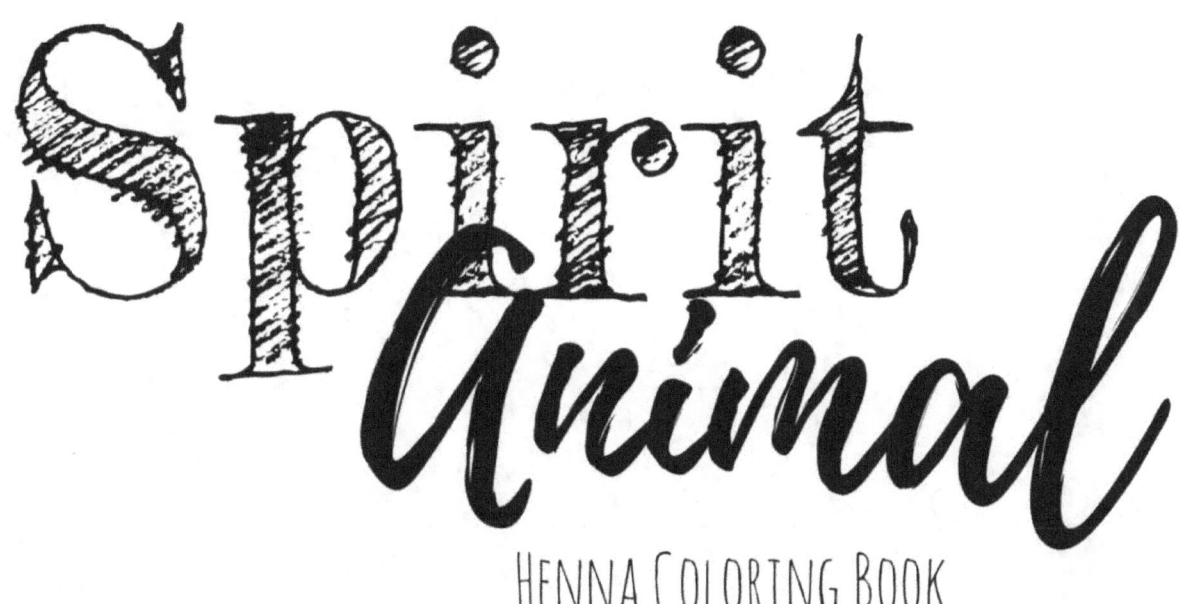

Spirit Animal
Henna Coloring Book

kathleen hennricks

Copyright © 2018 Kathleen Hennricks
All rights reserved.
ISBN: 1985837358
ISBN-13:978-1985837355

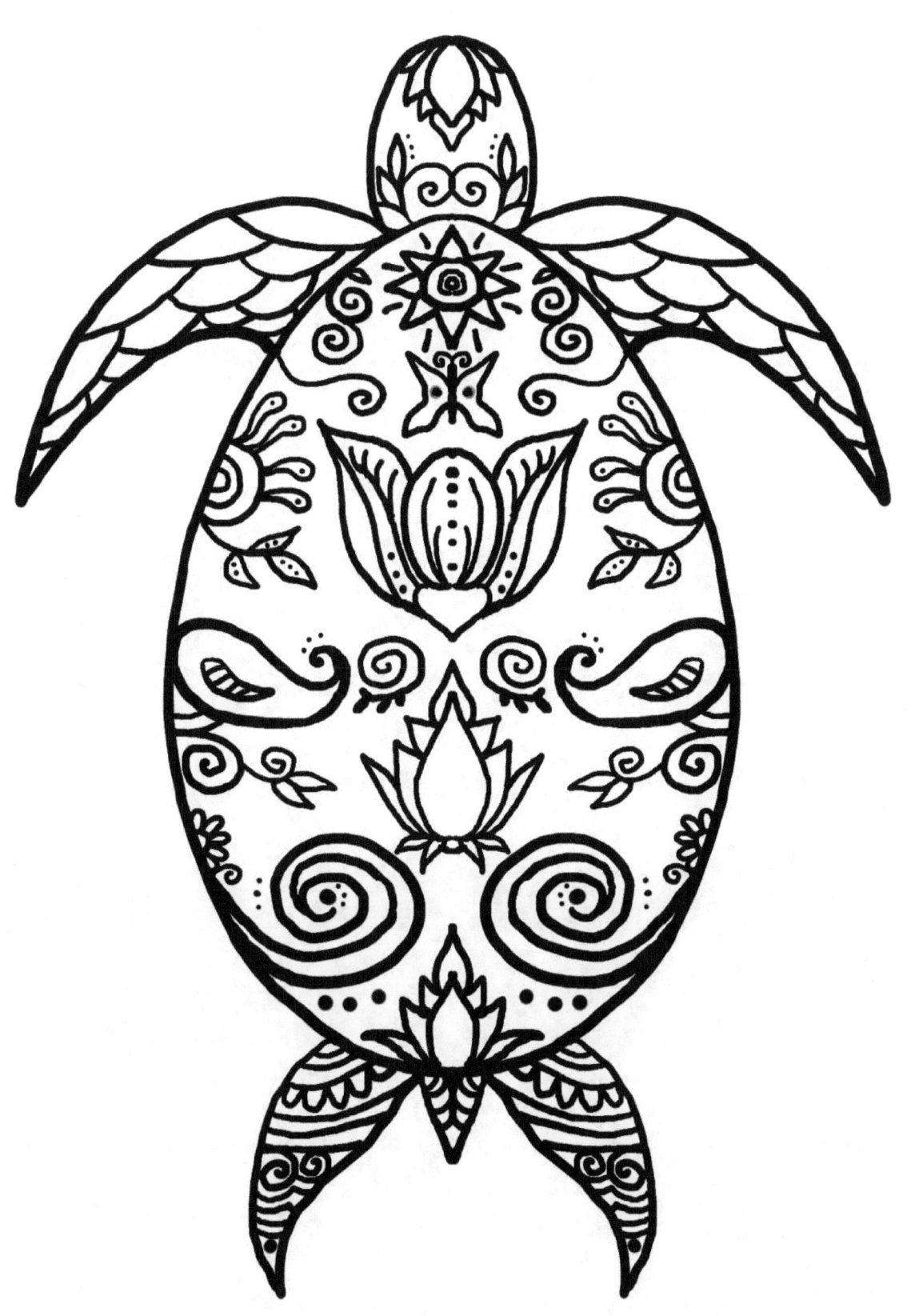

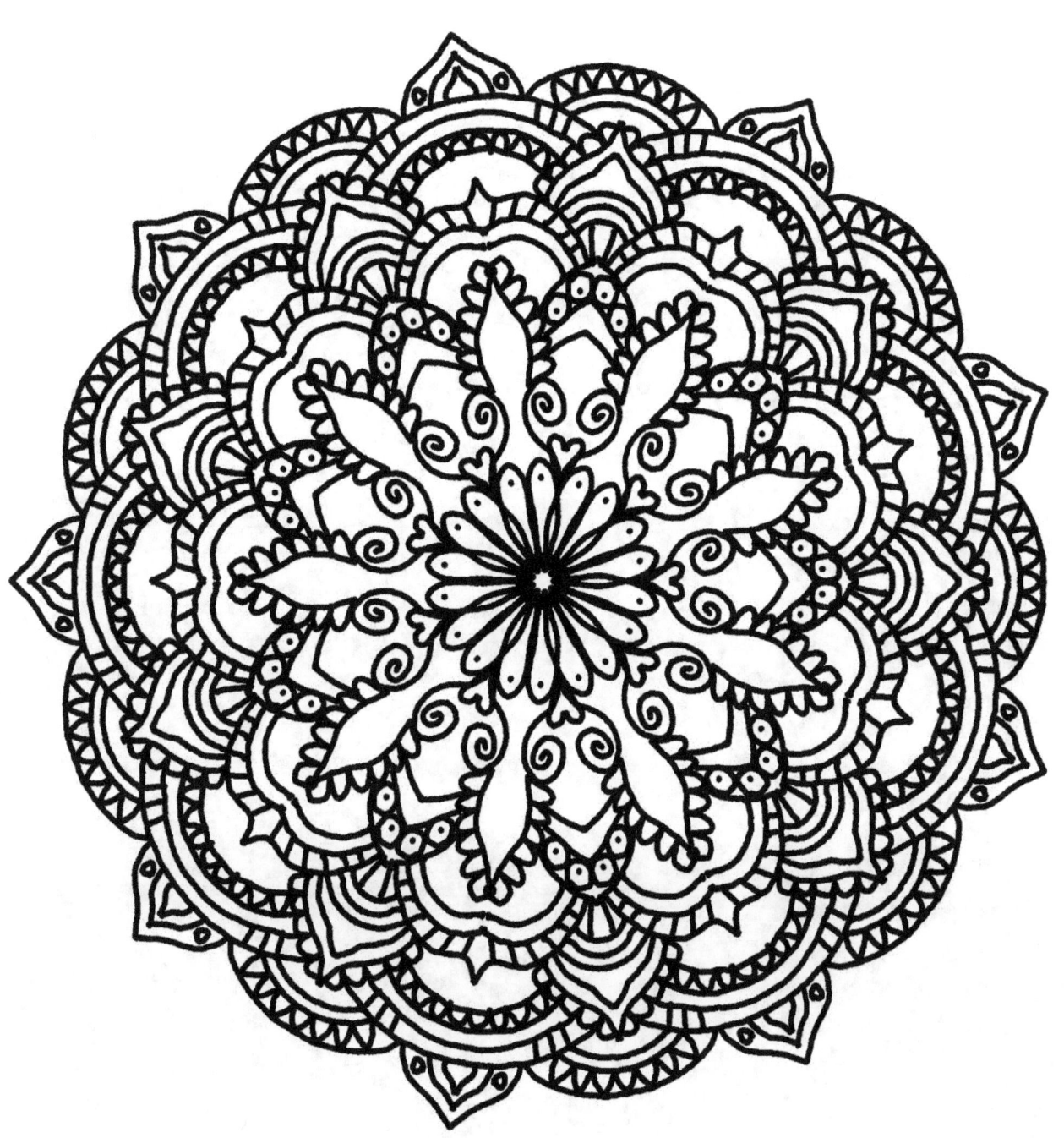

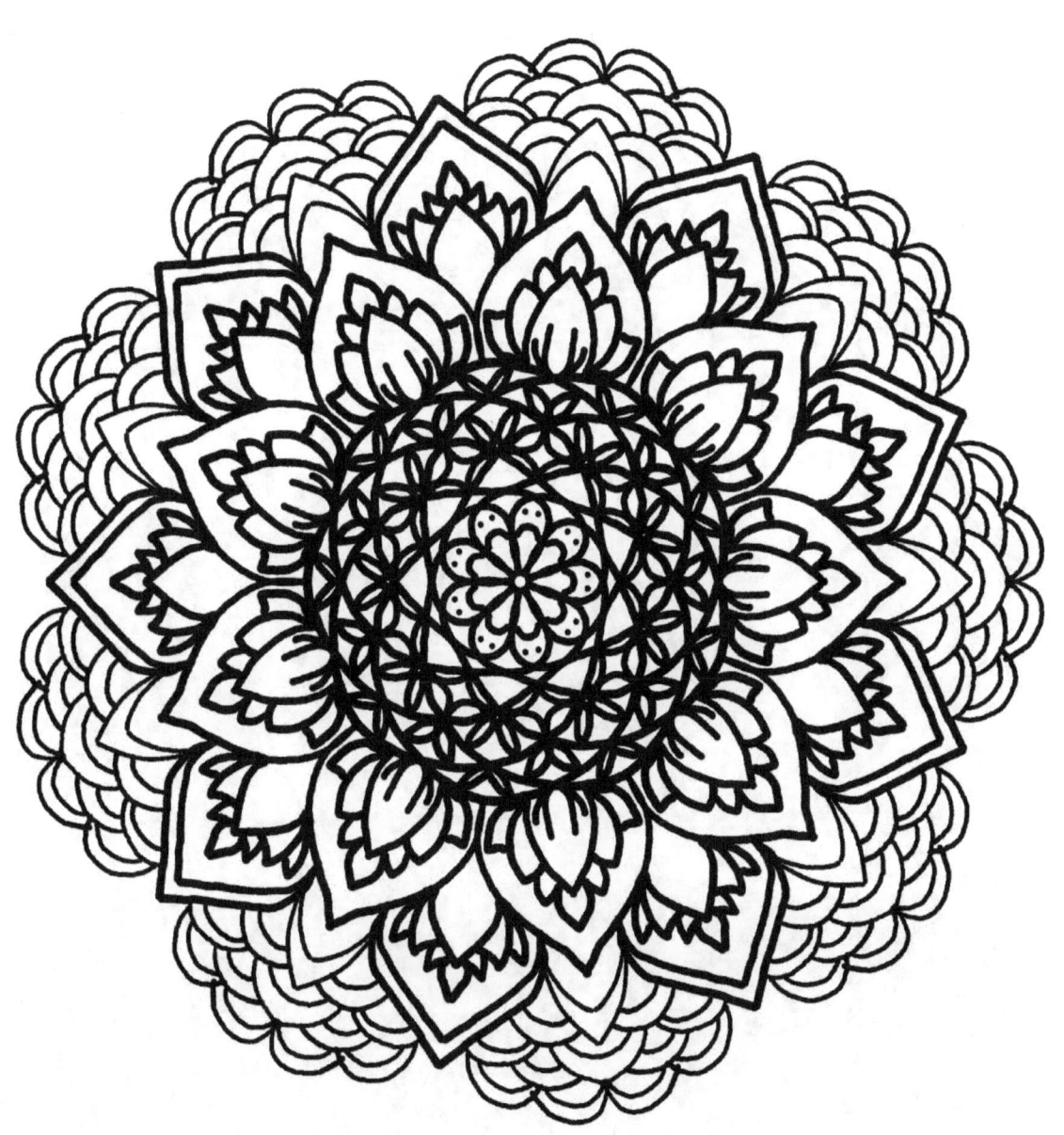

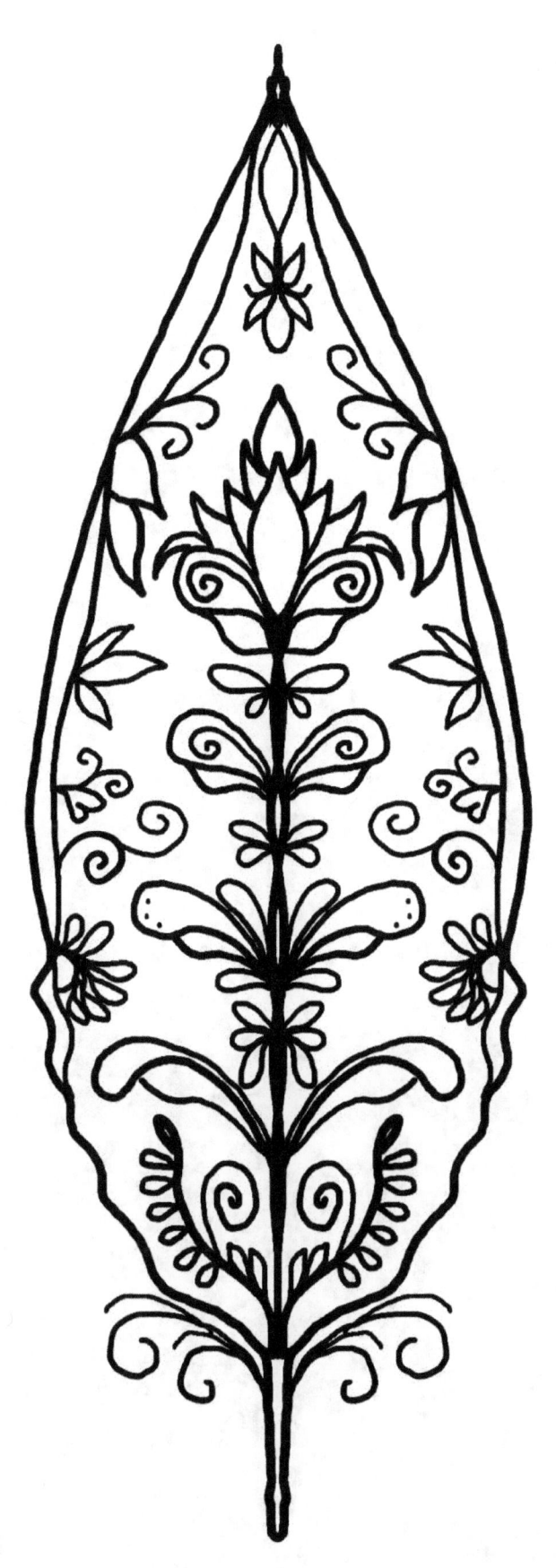

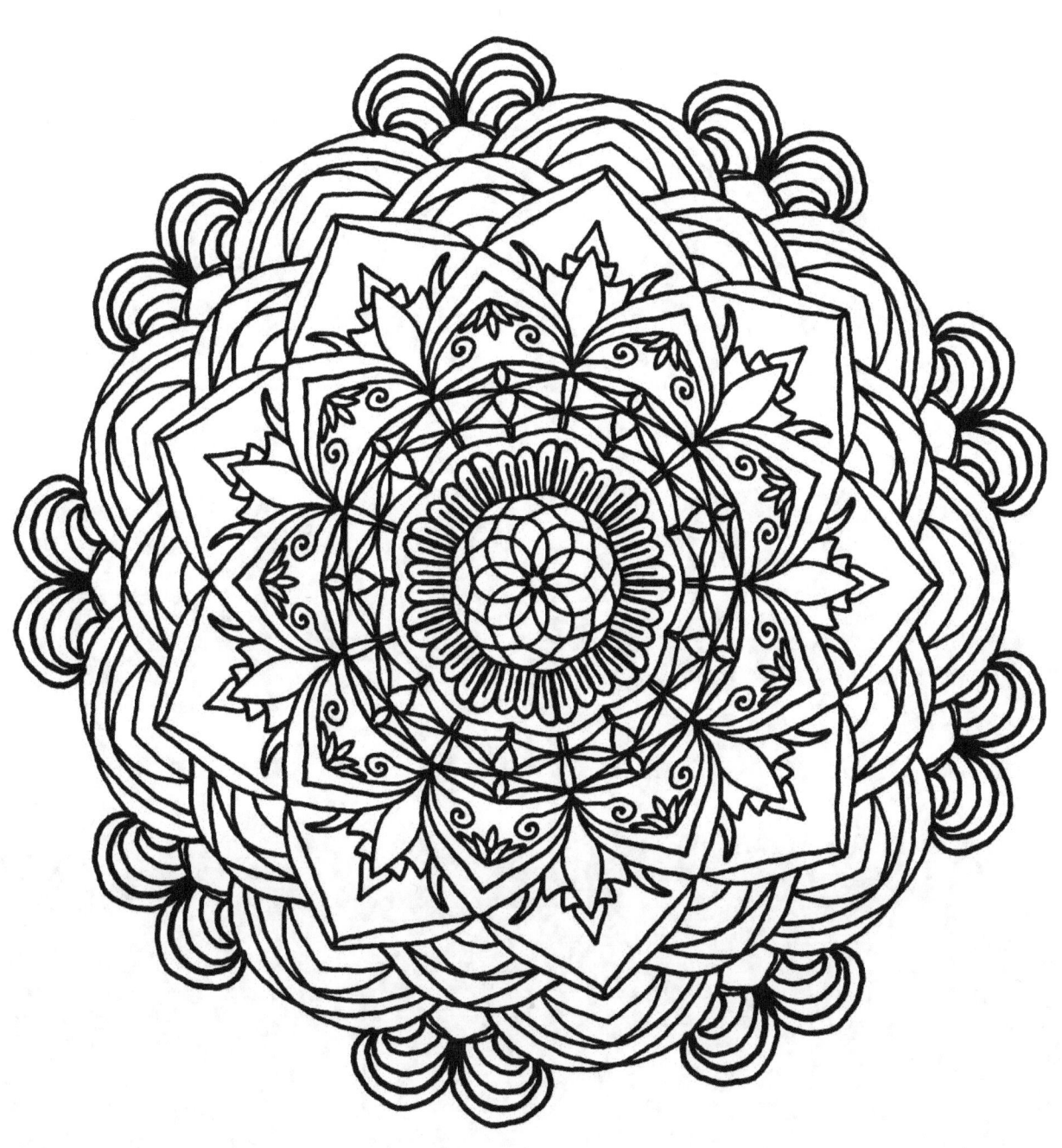

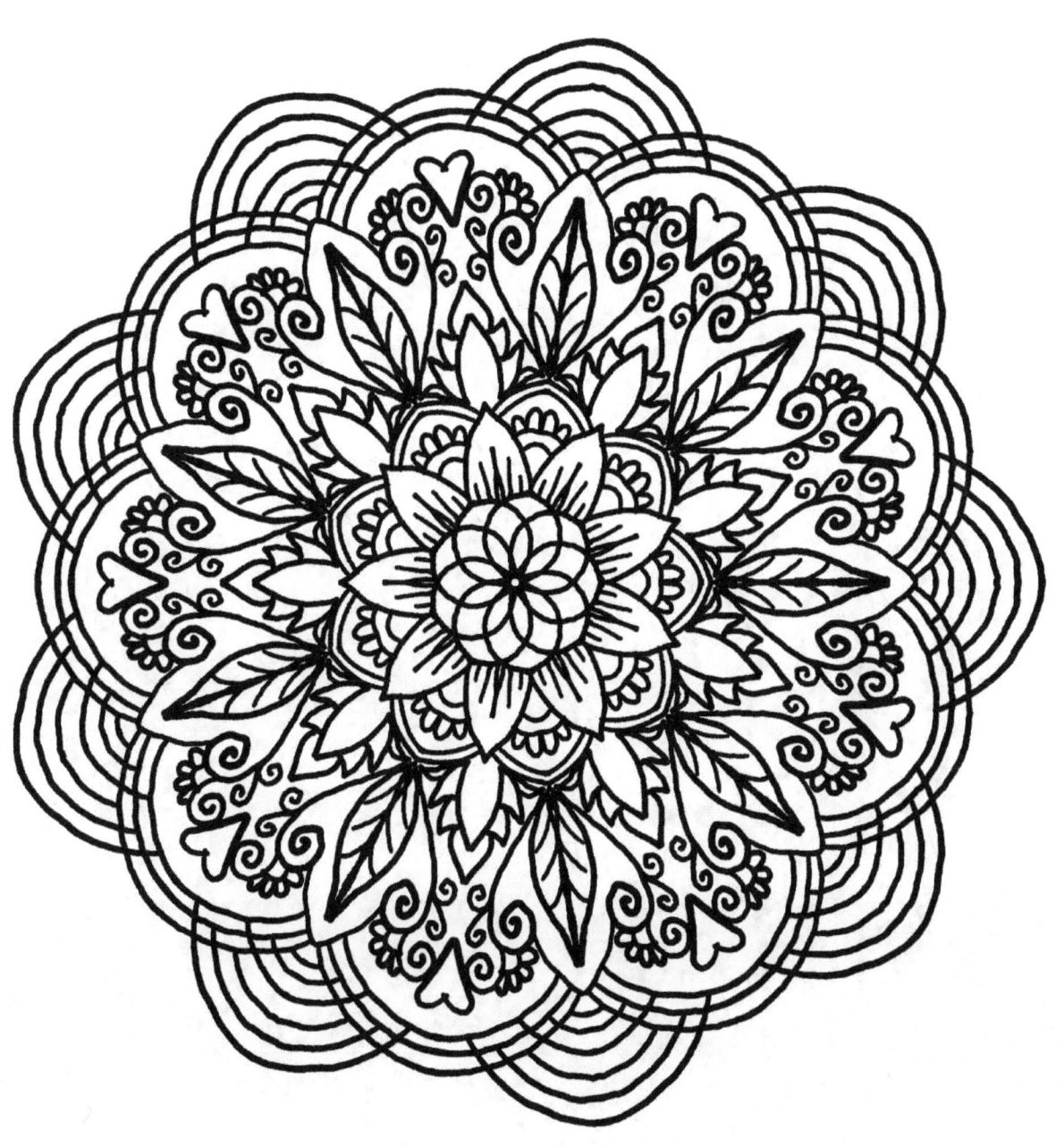

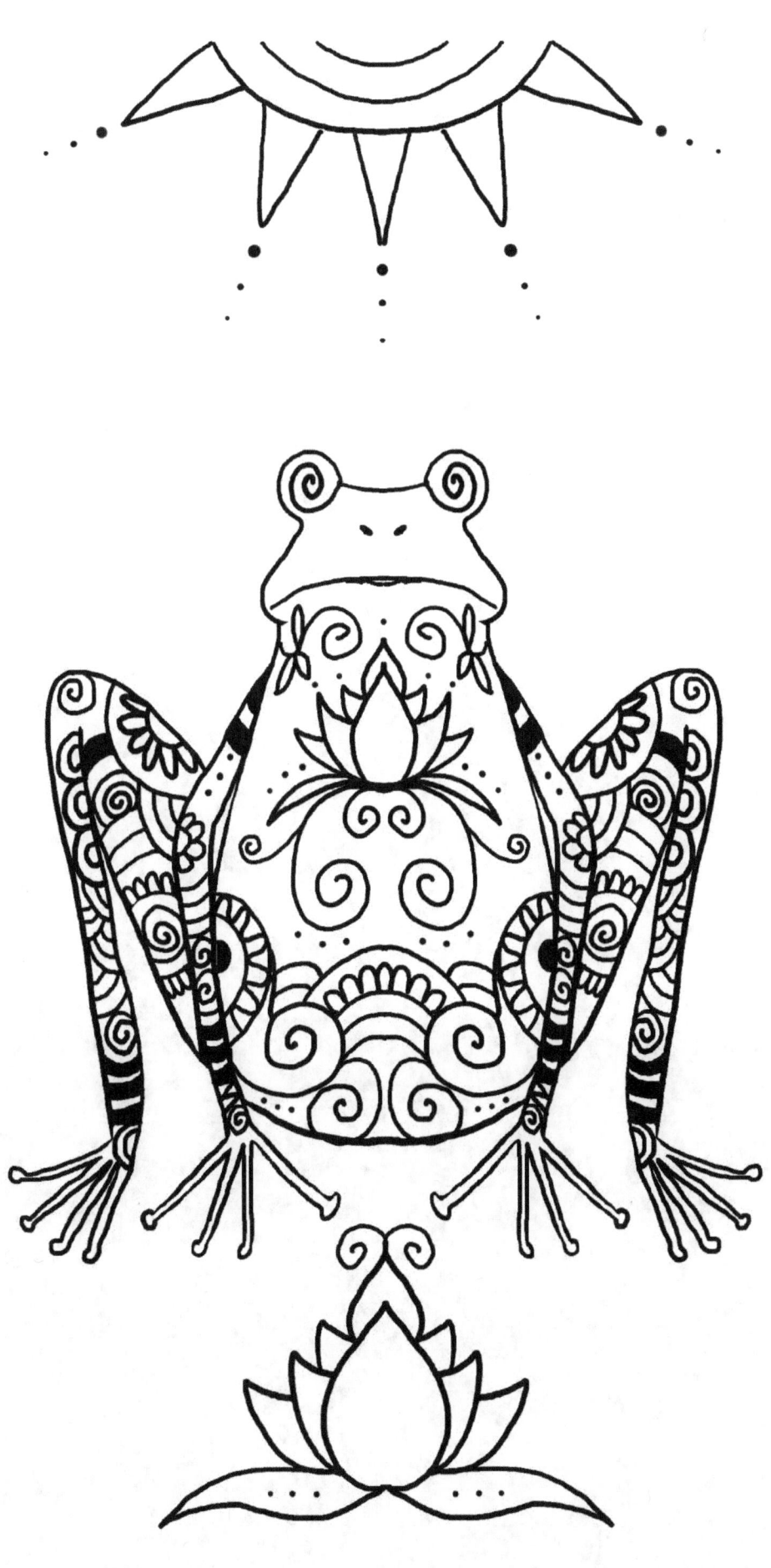

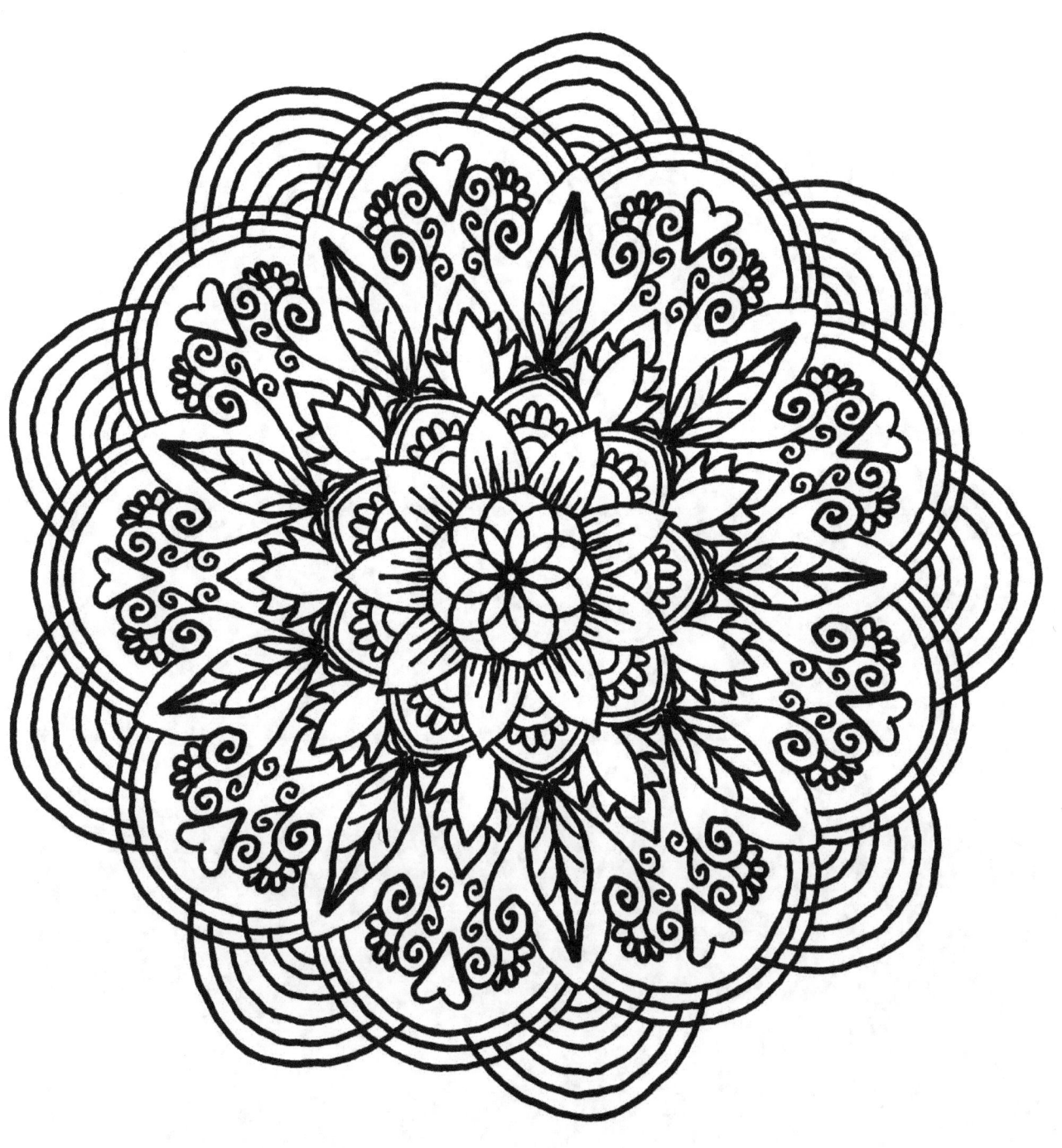

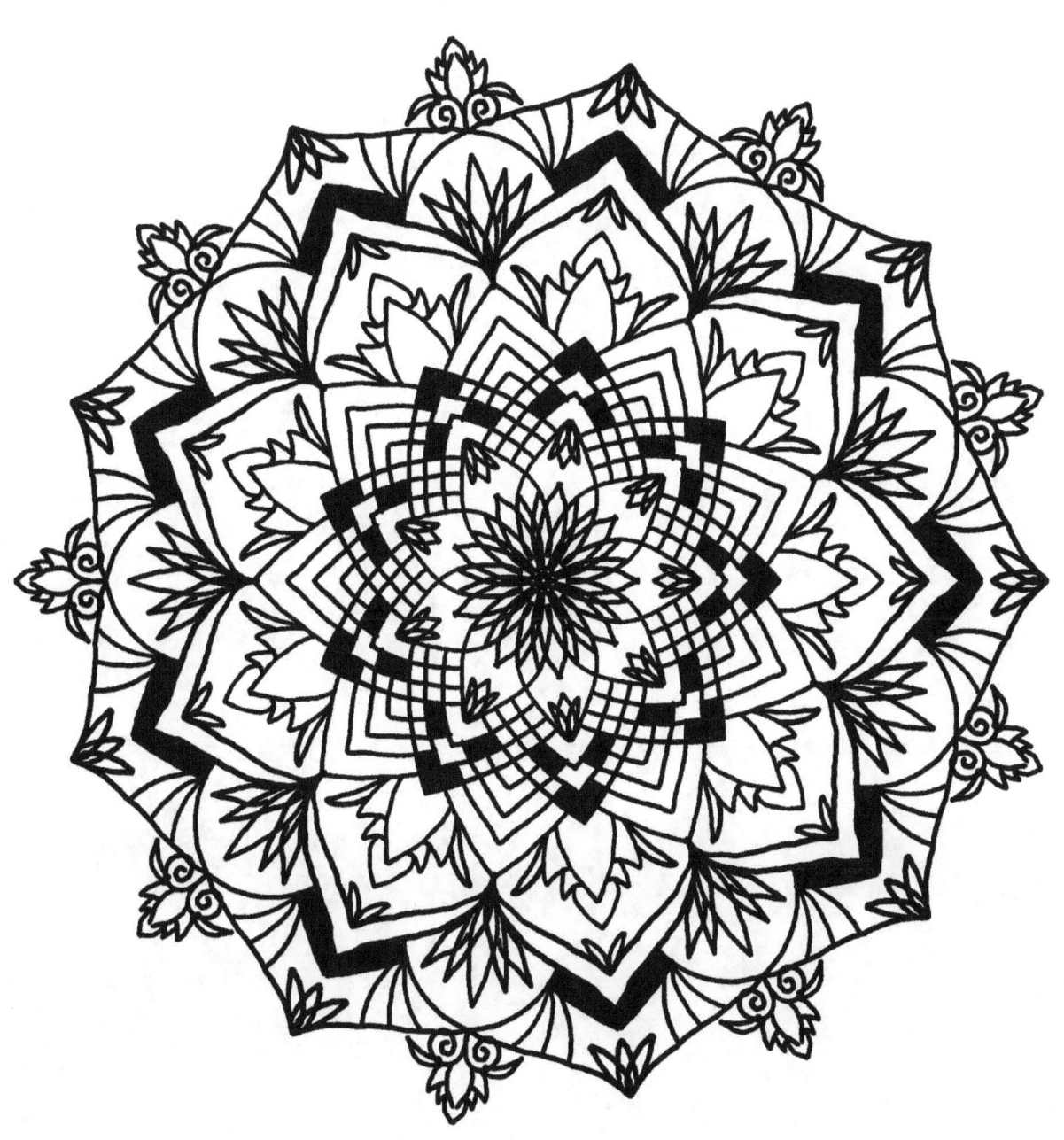

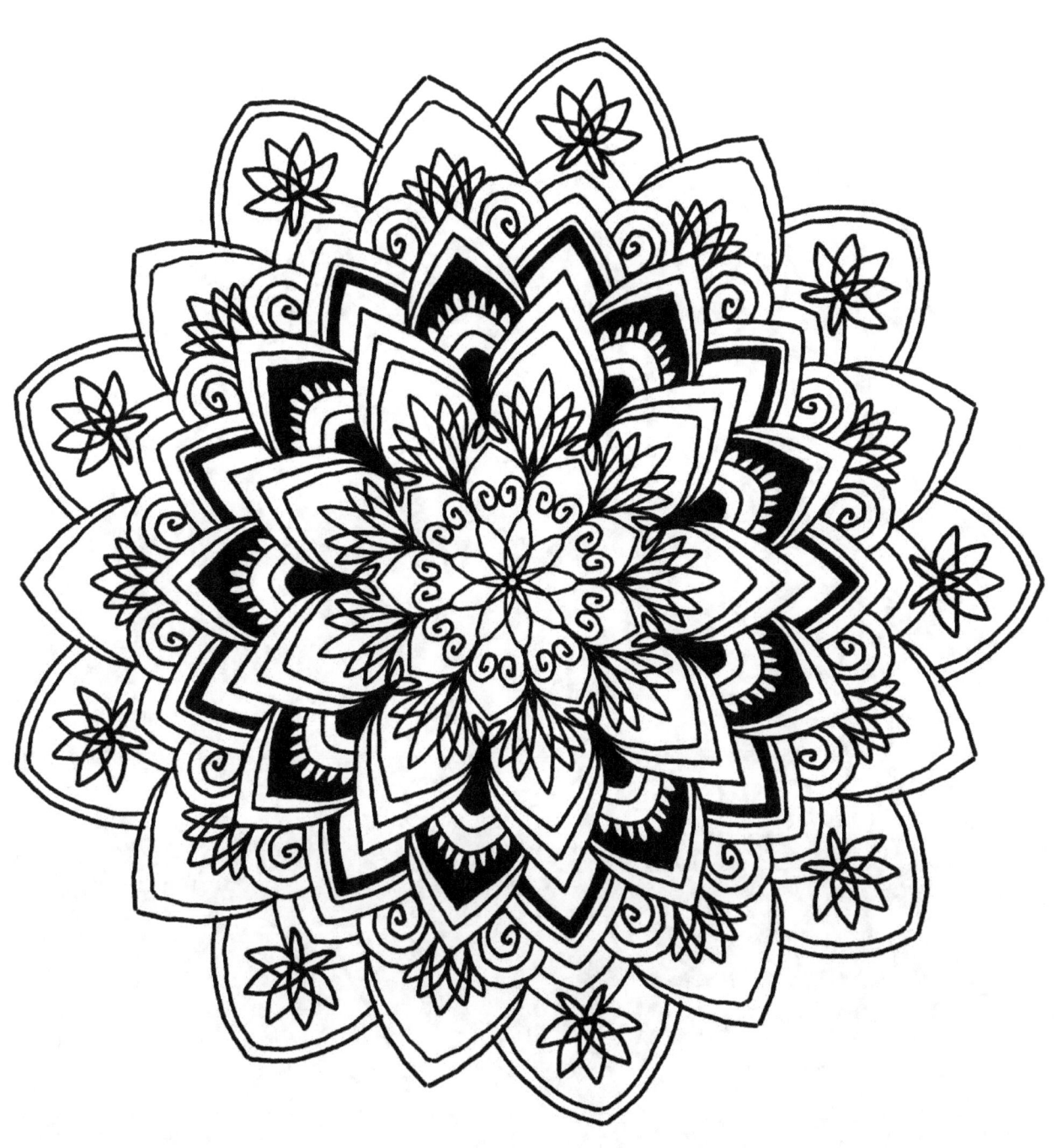

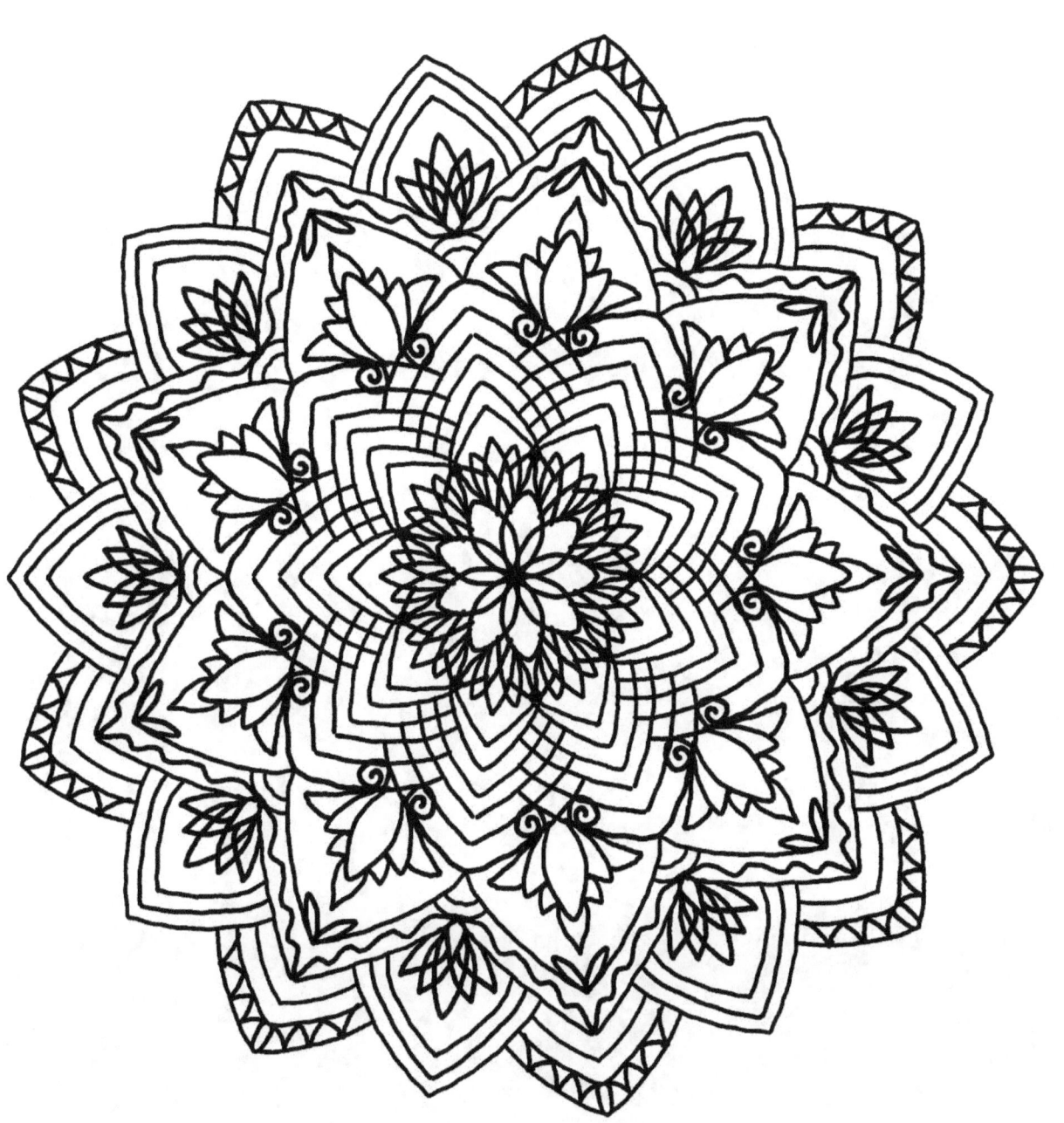

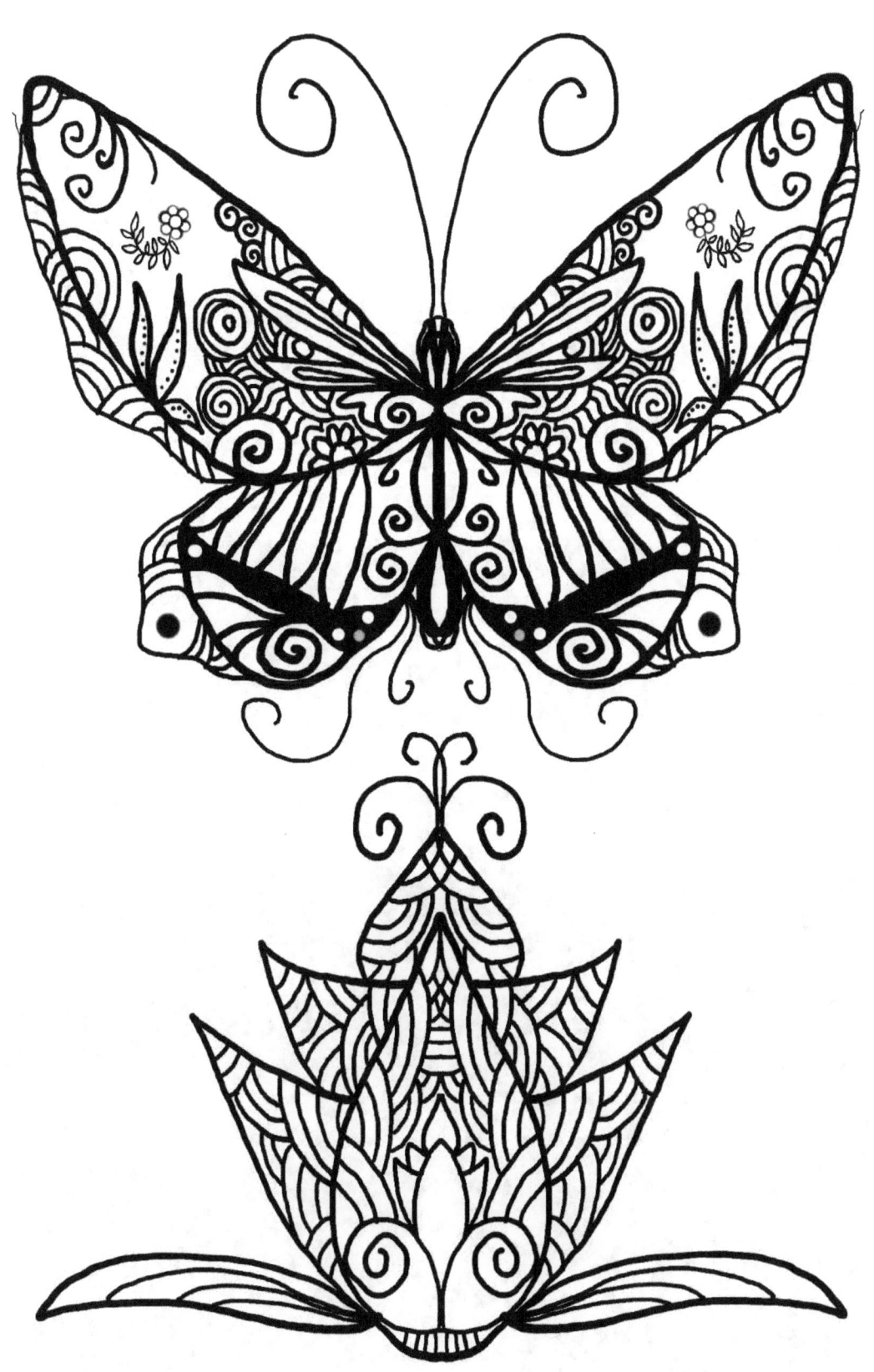

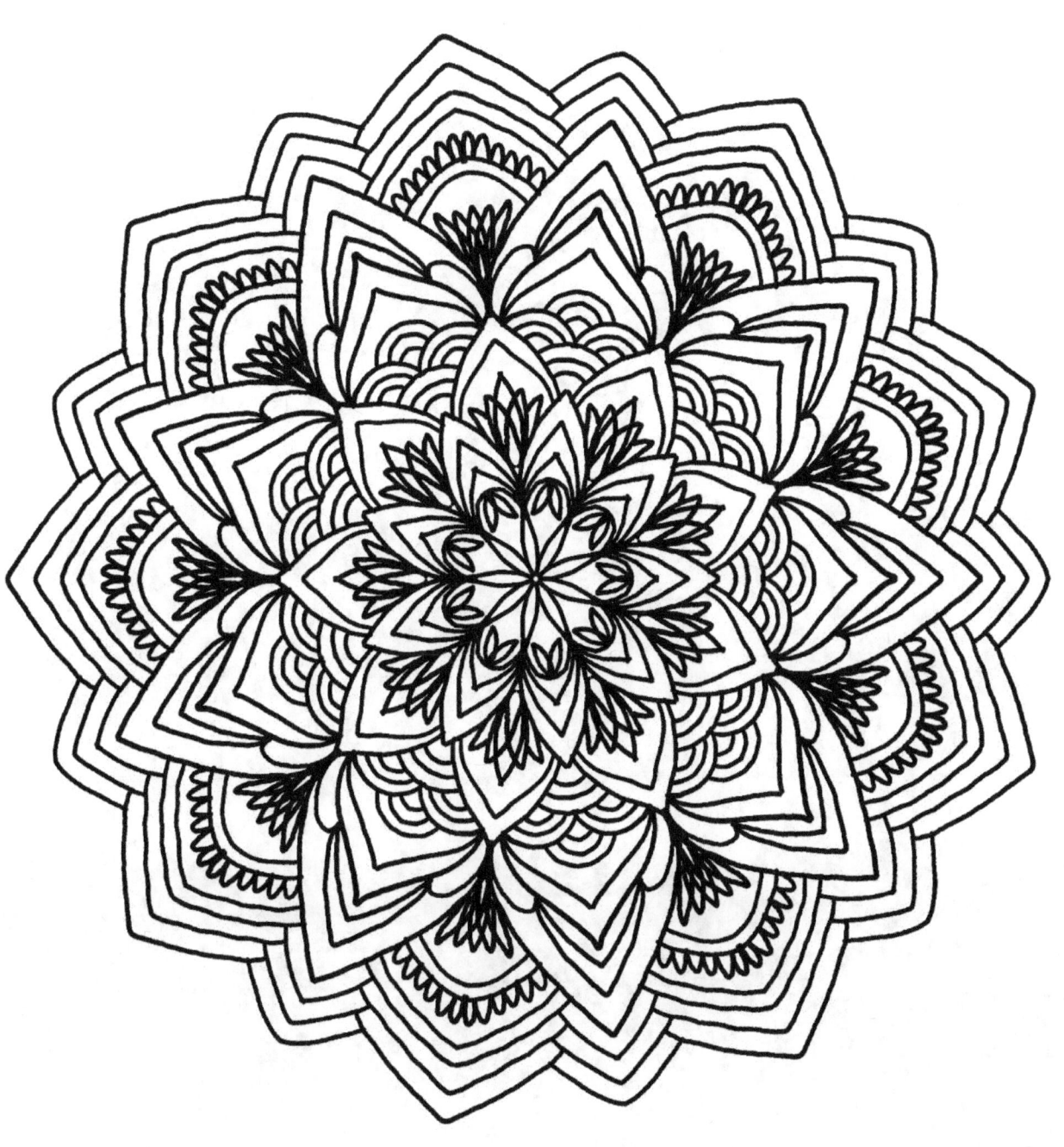

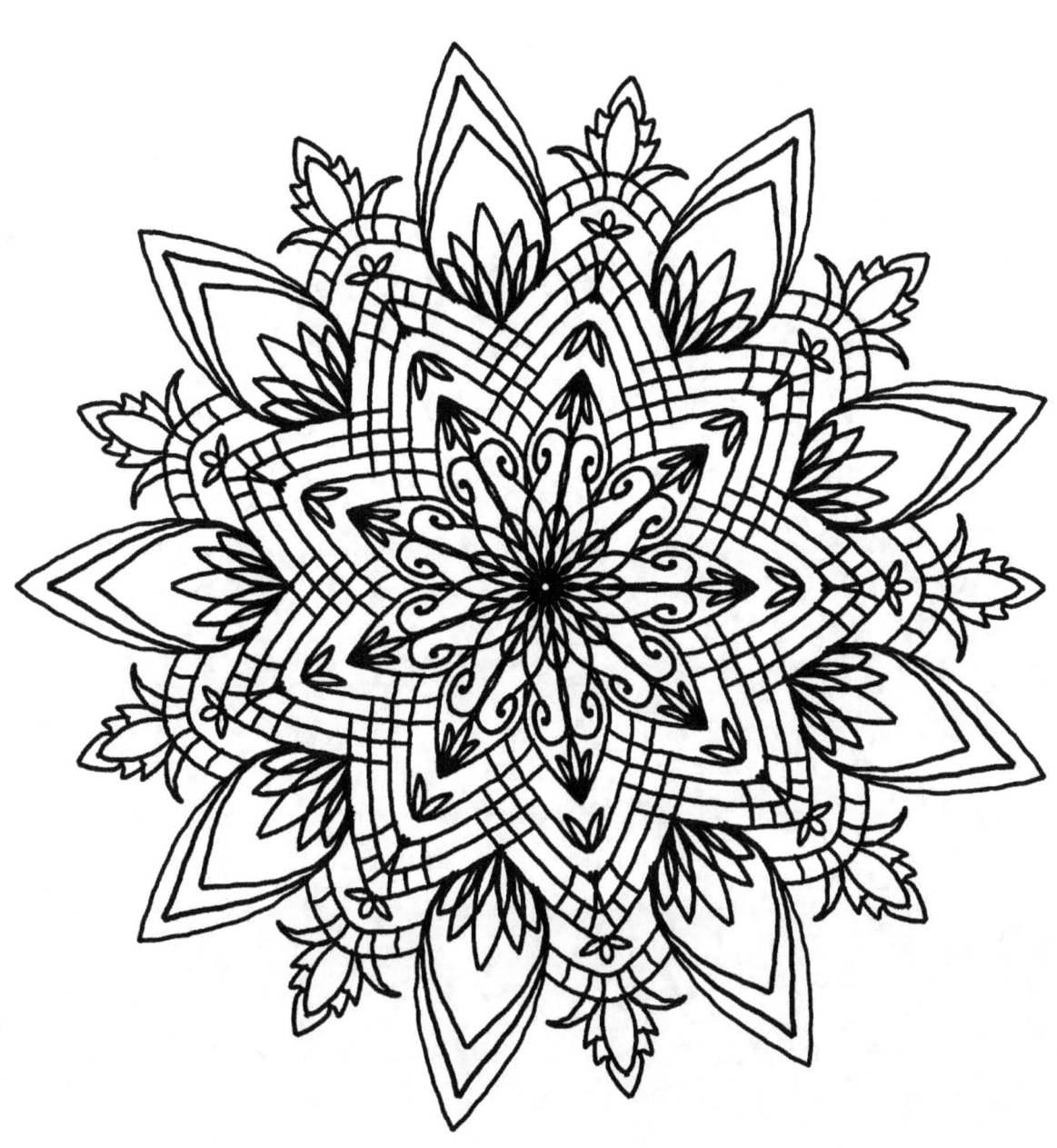

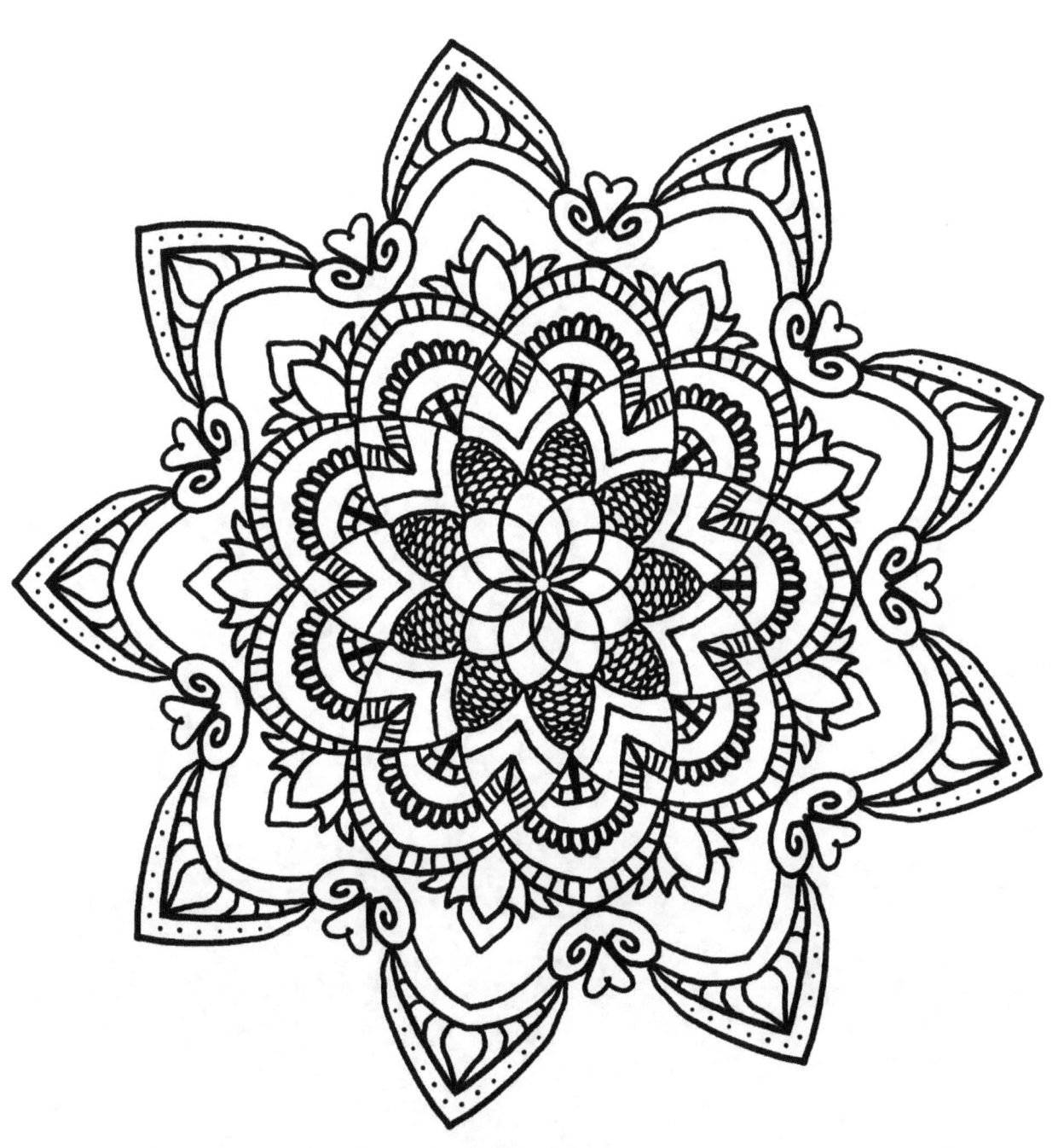

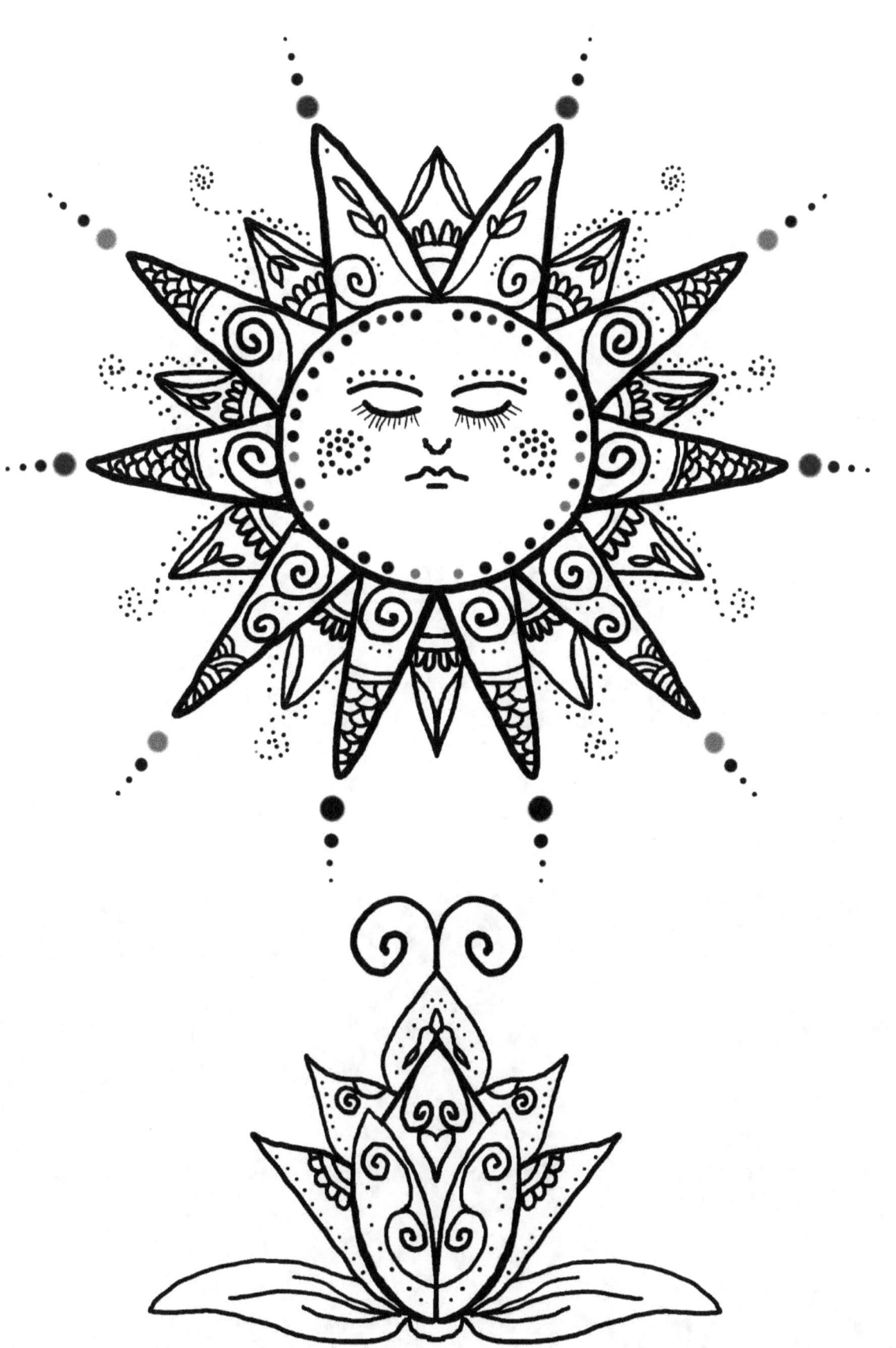

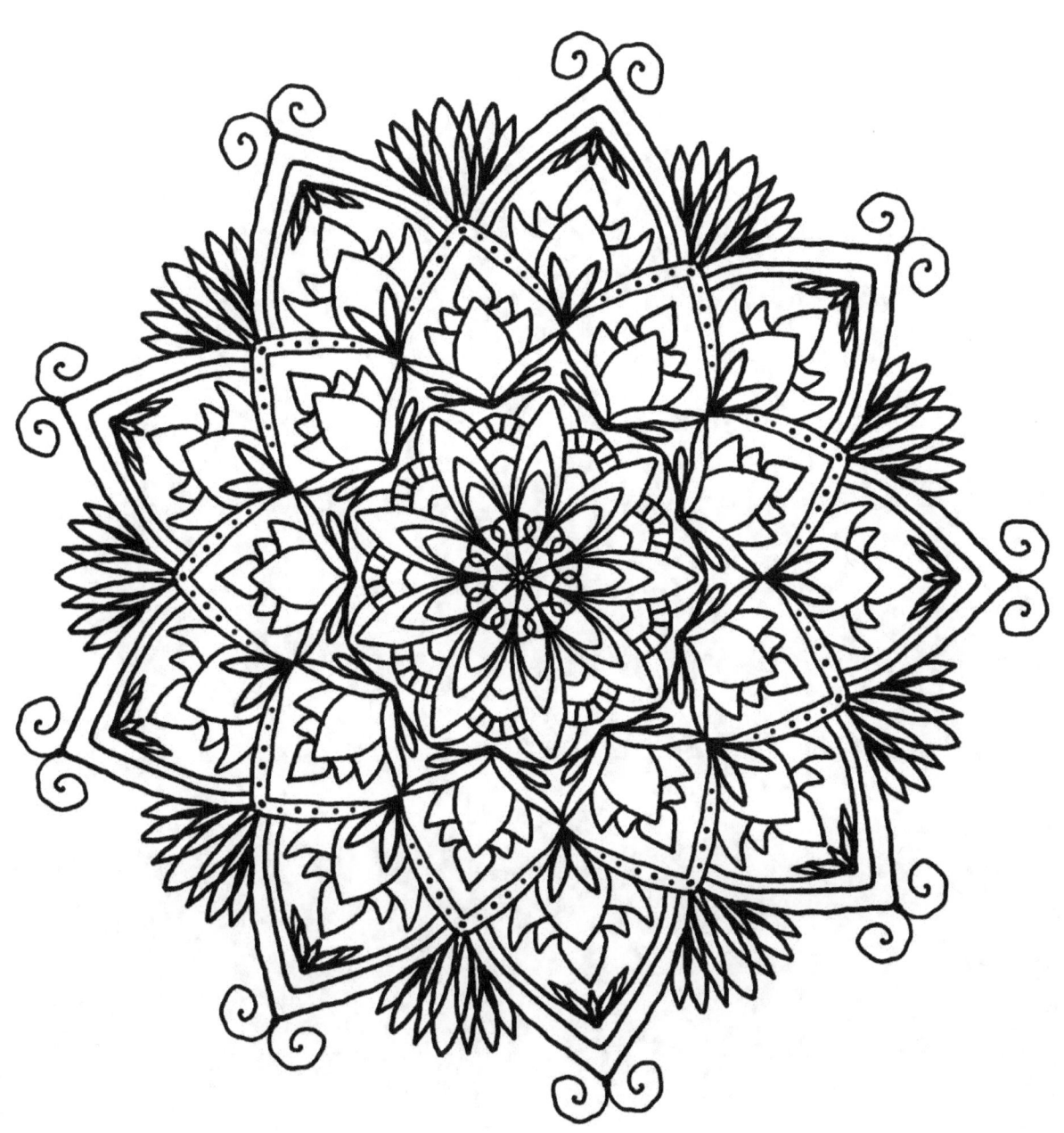

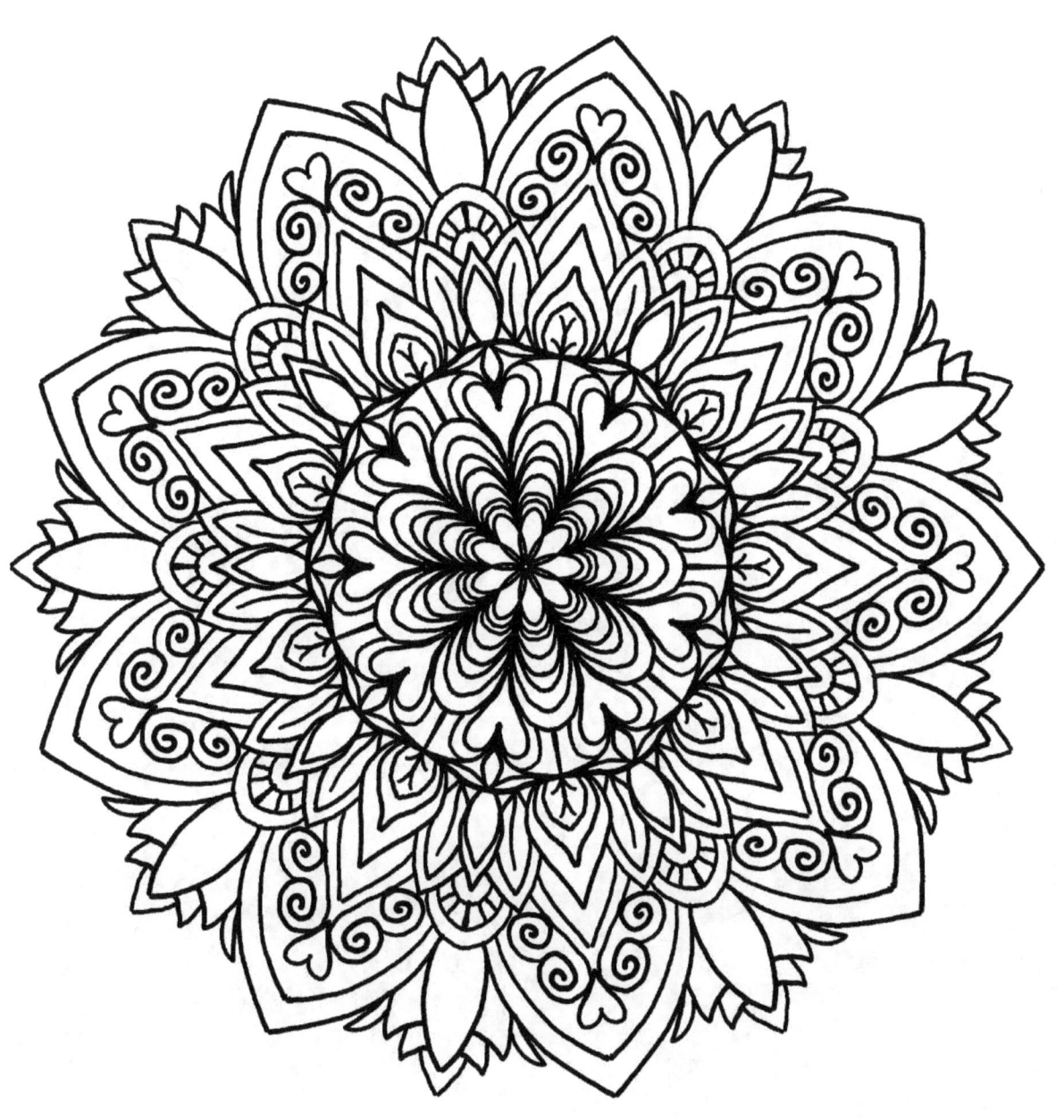

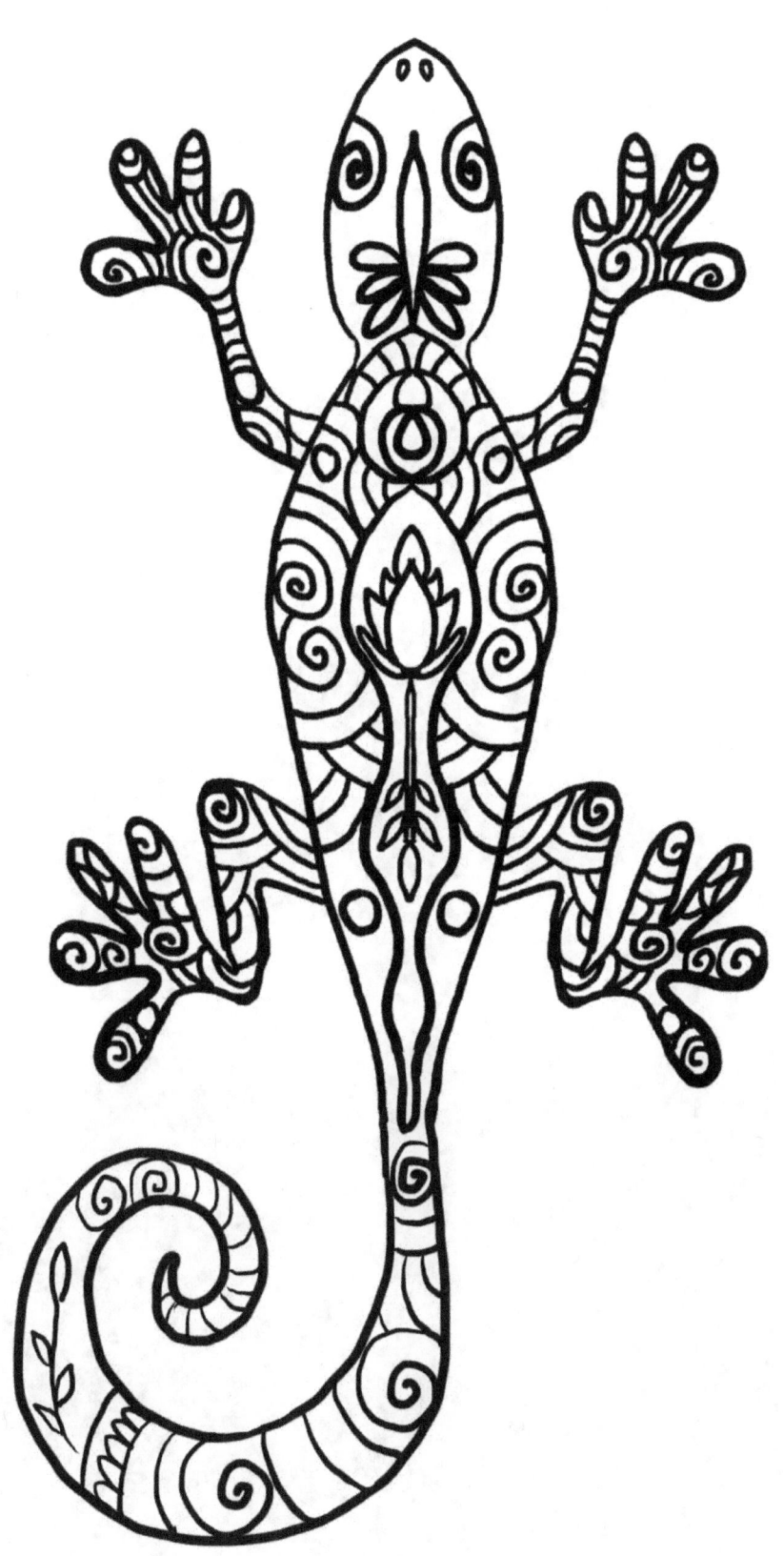

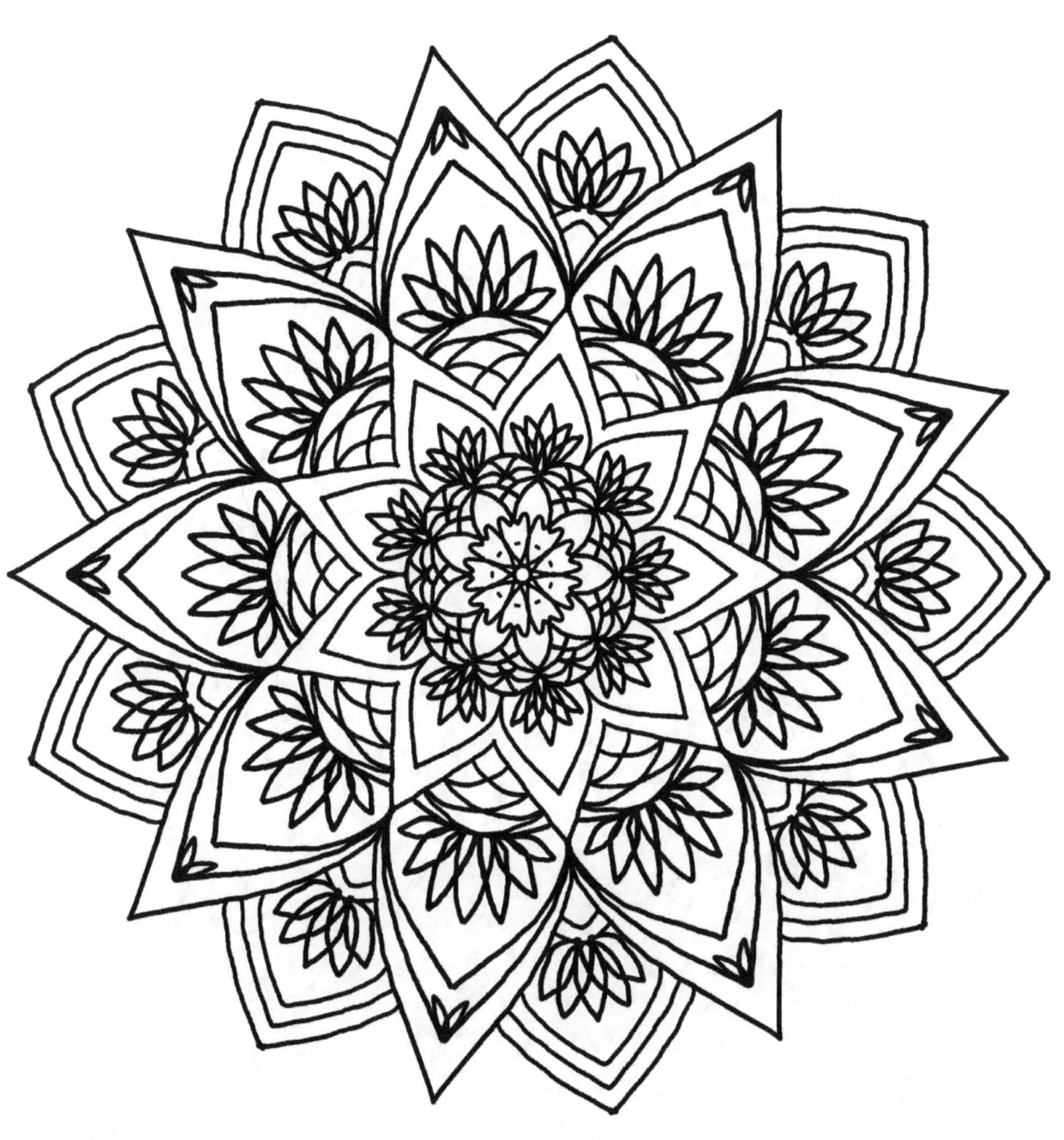

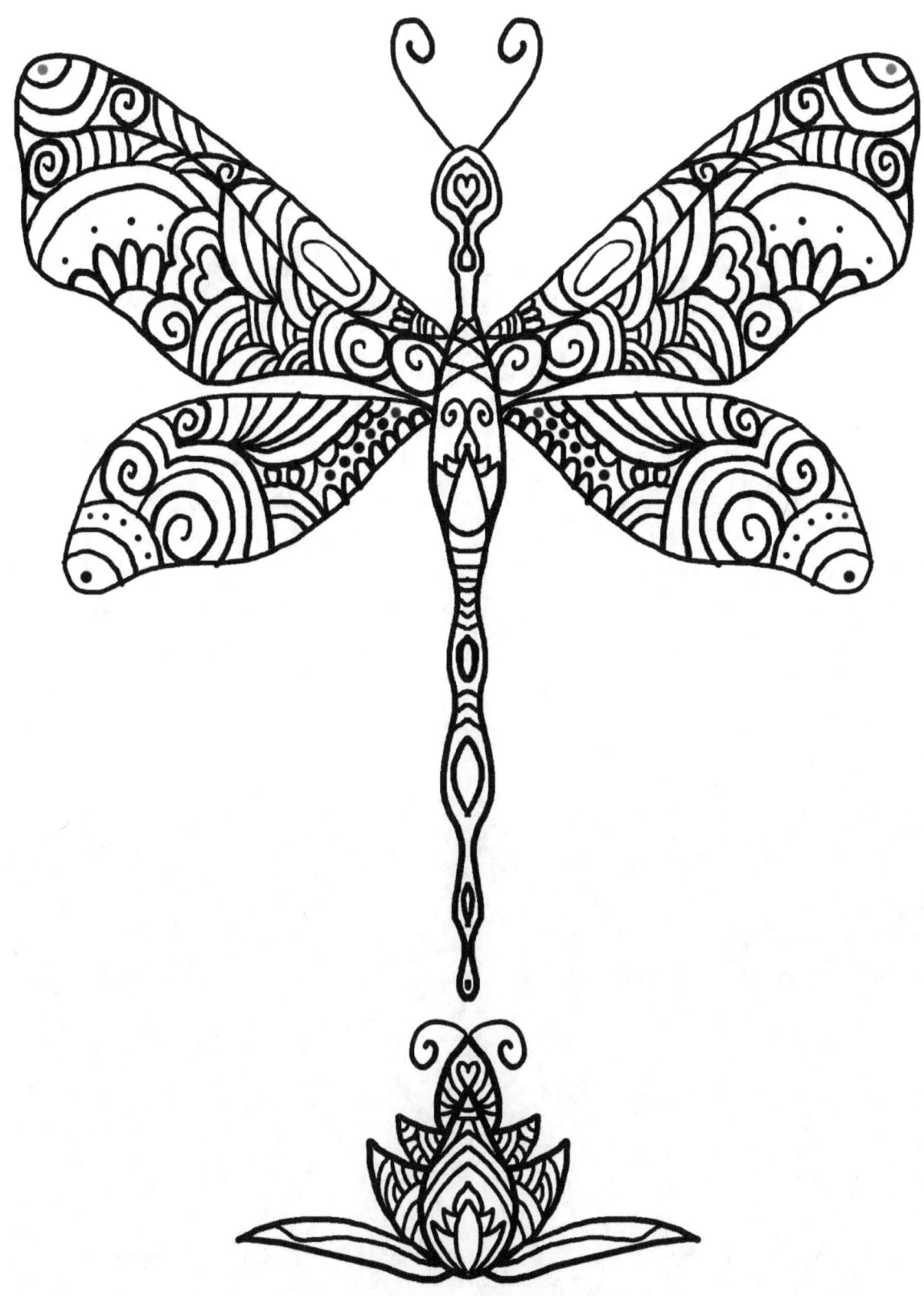

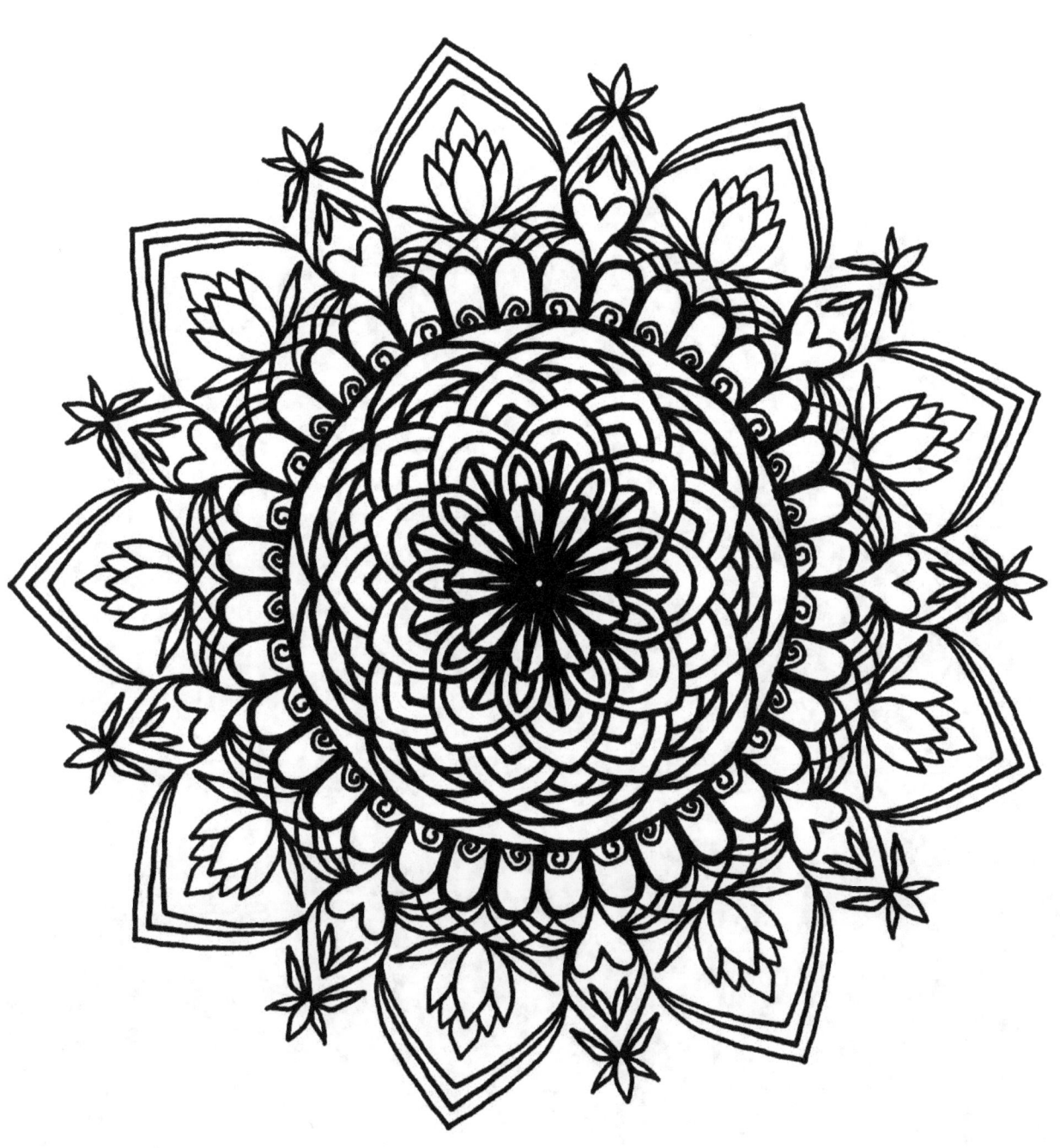

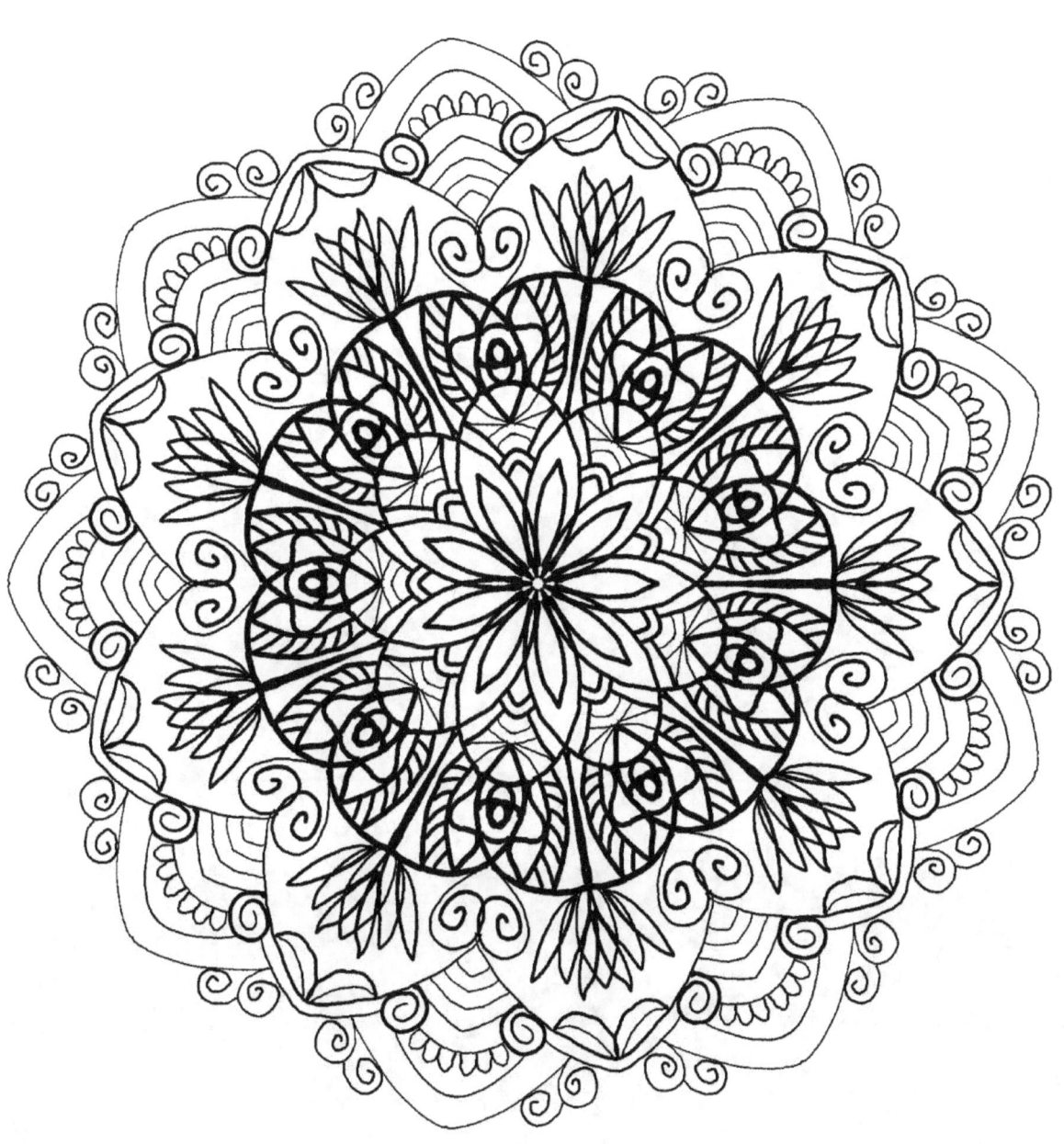

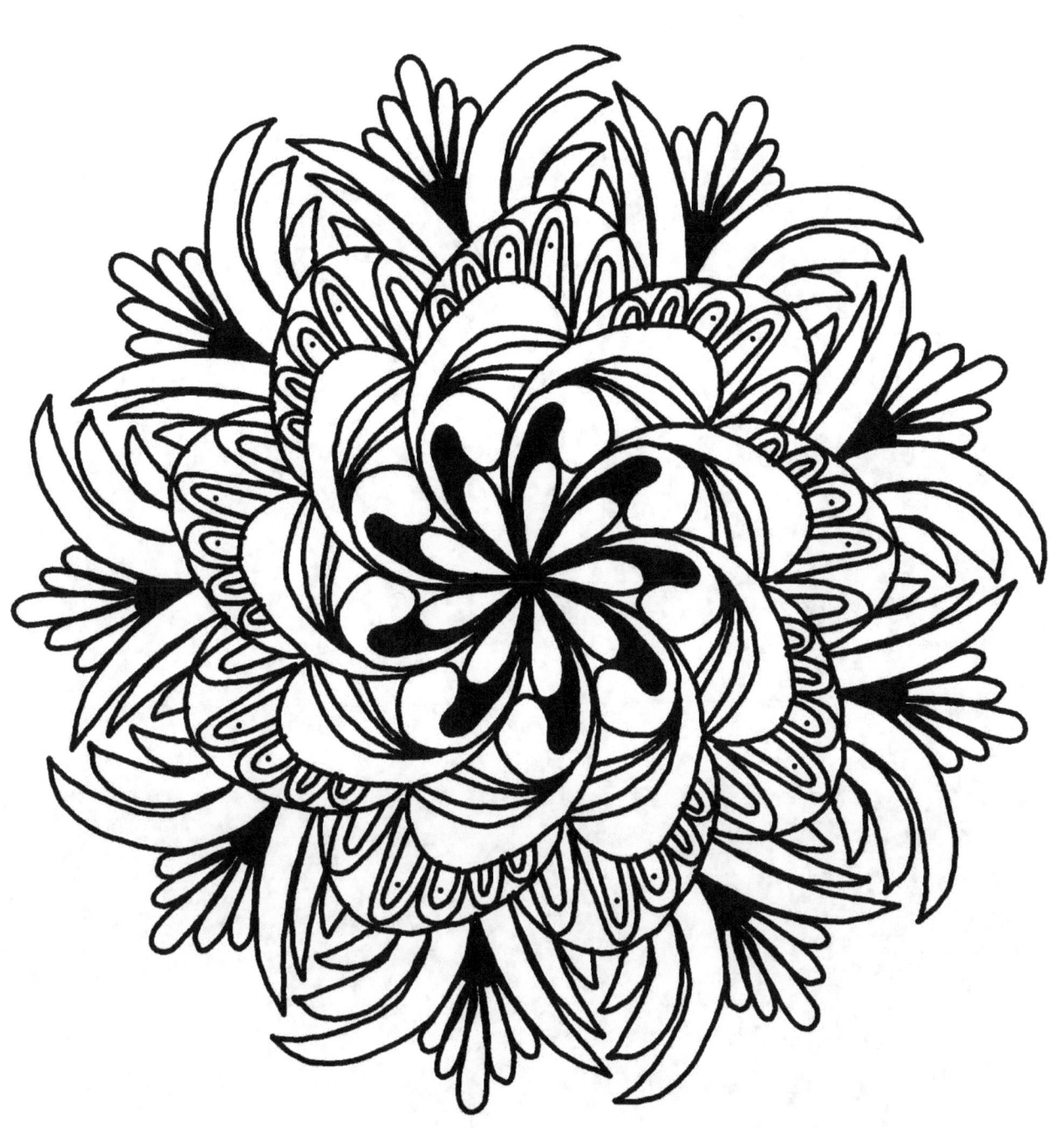

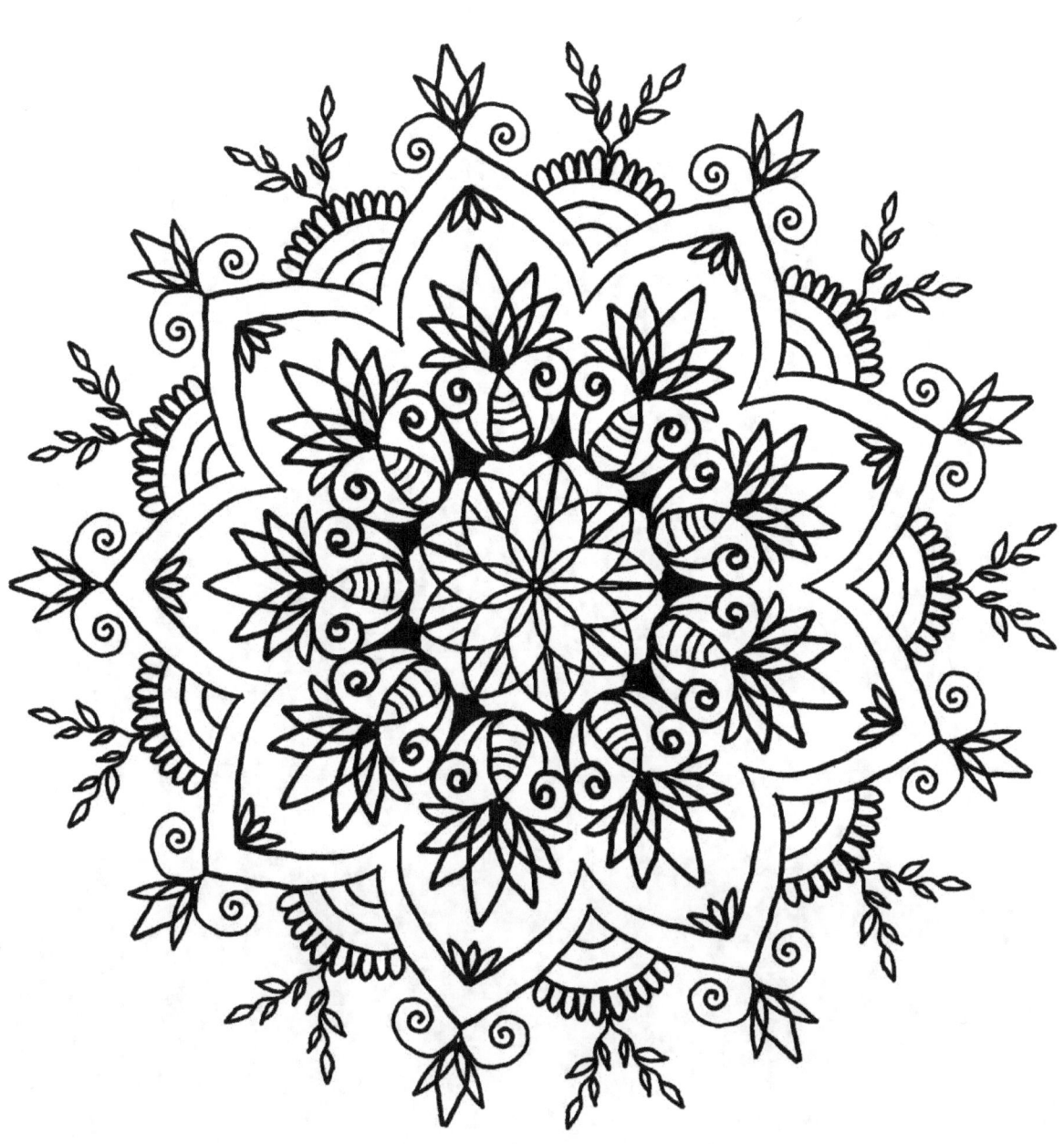

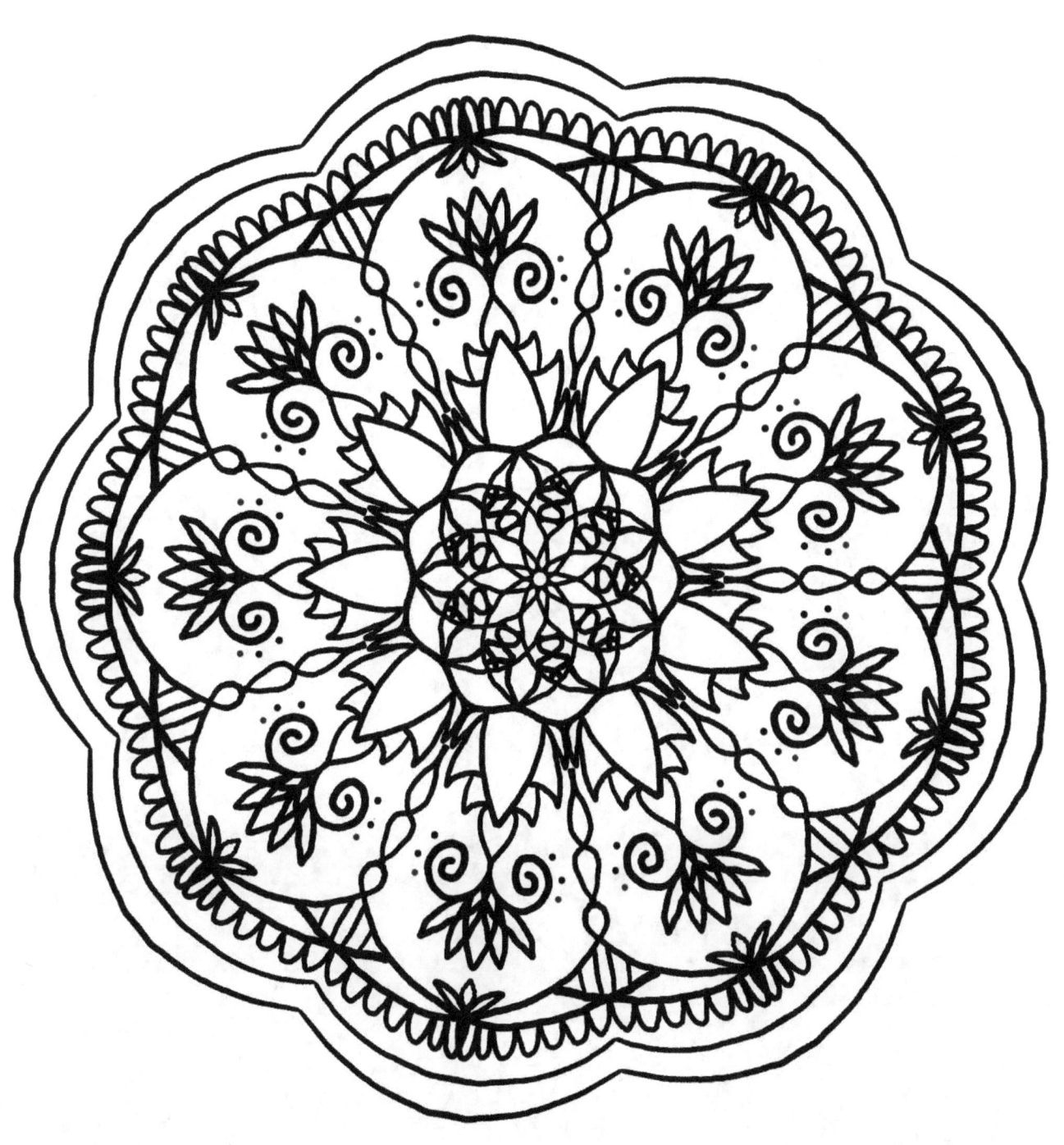

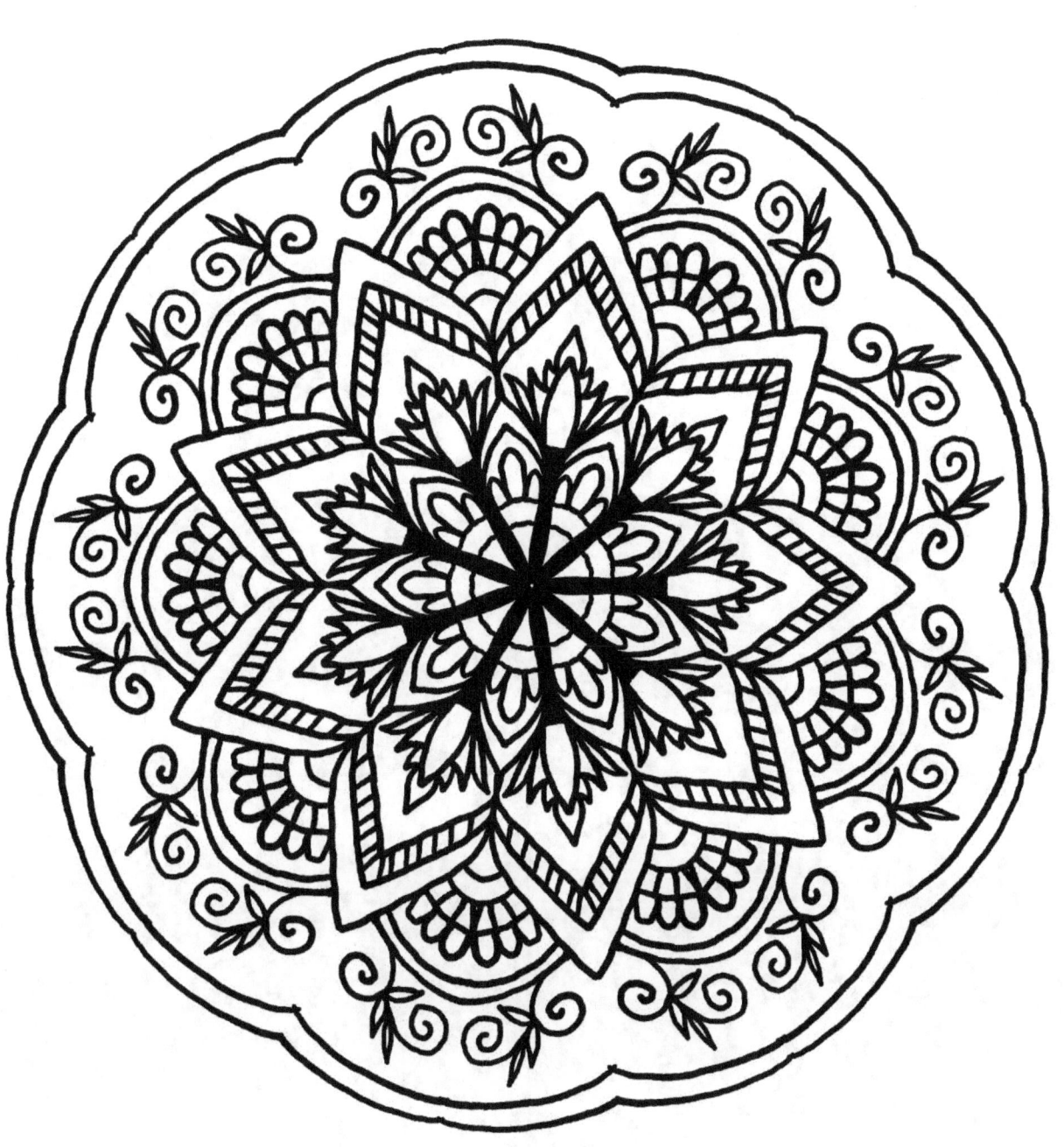

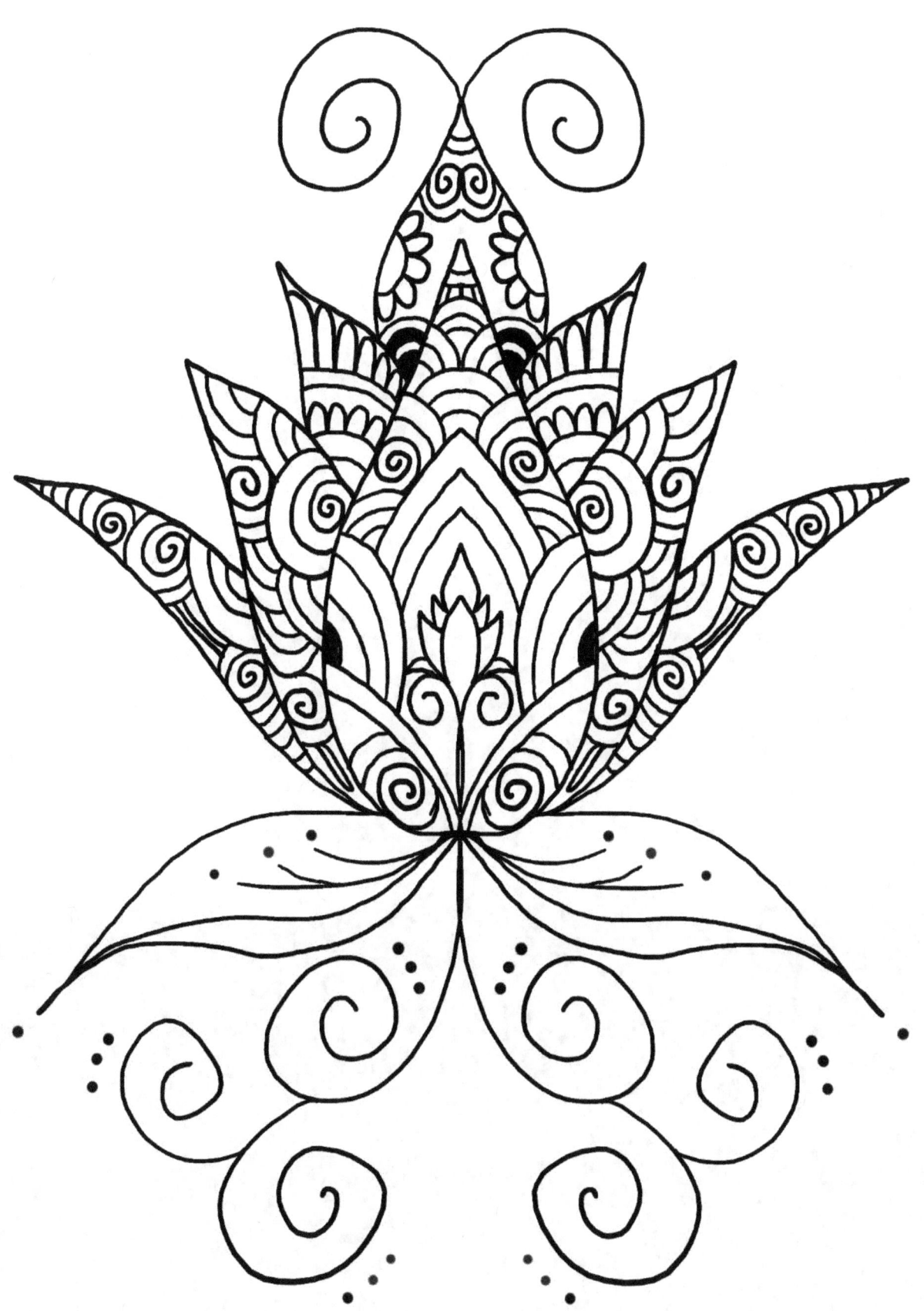

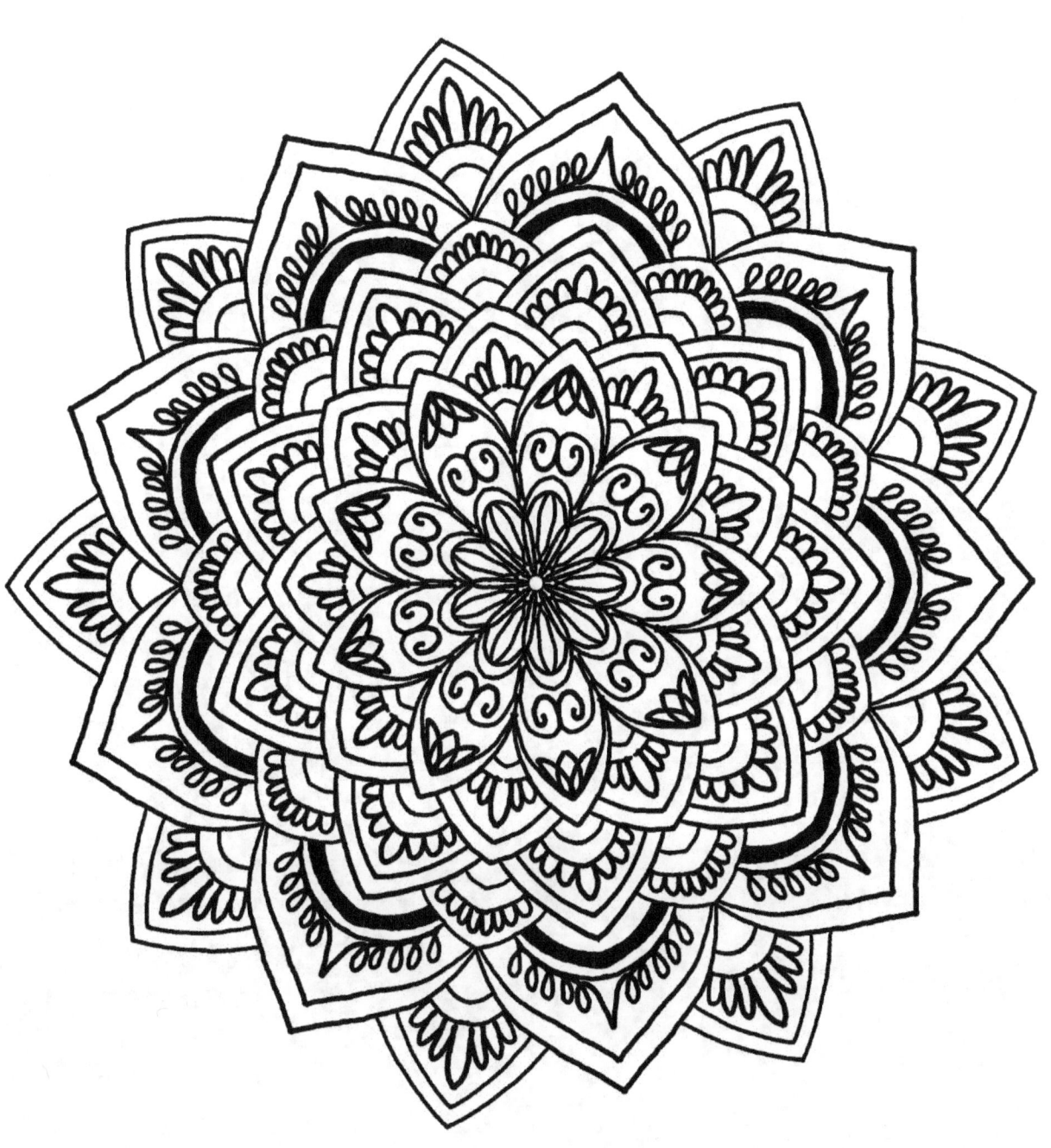

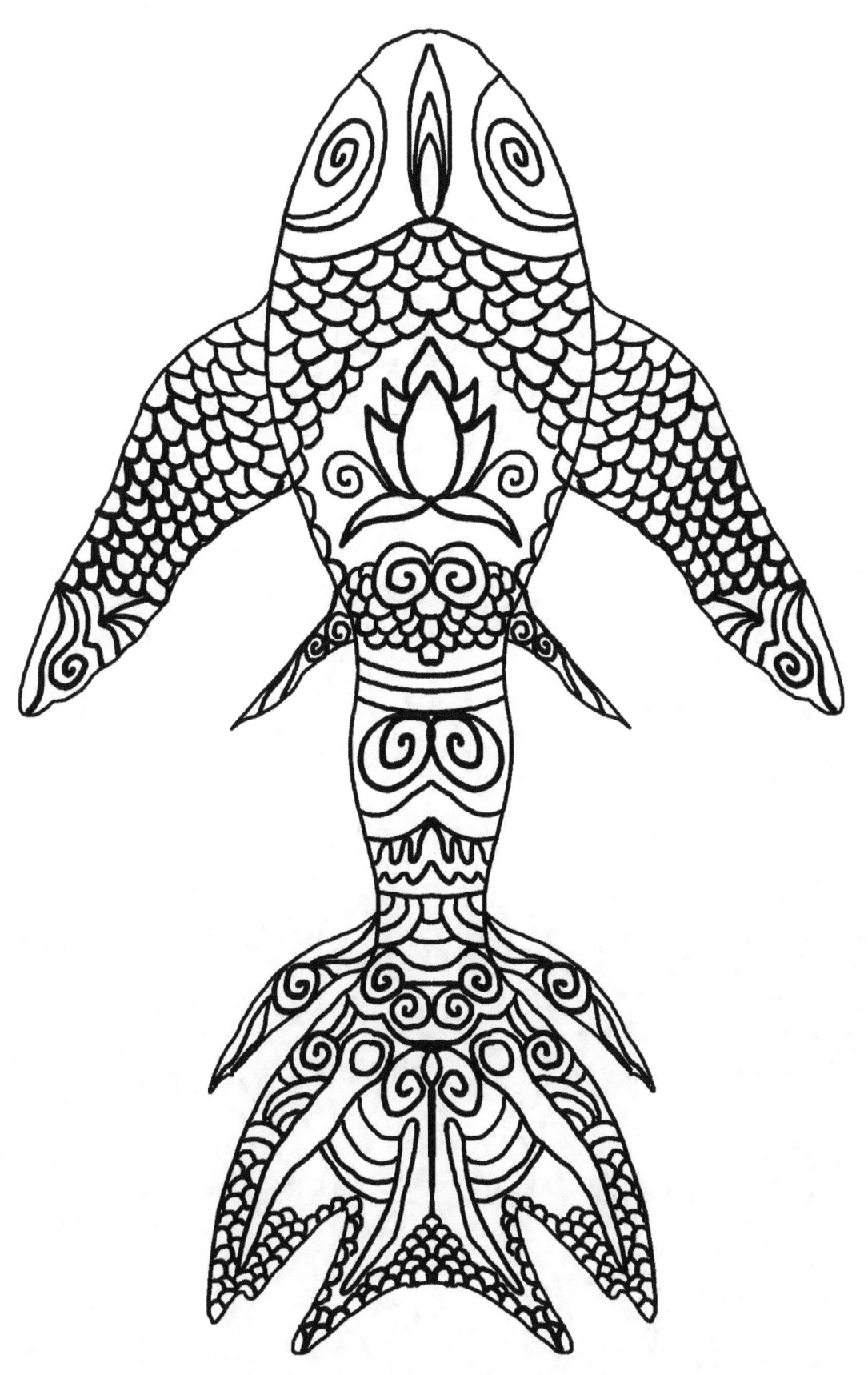

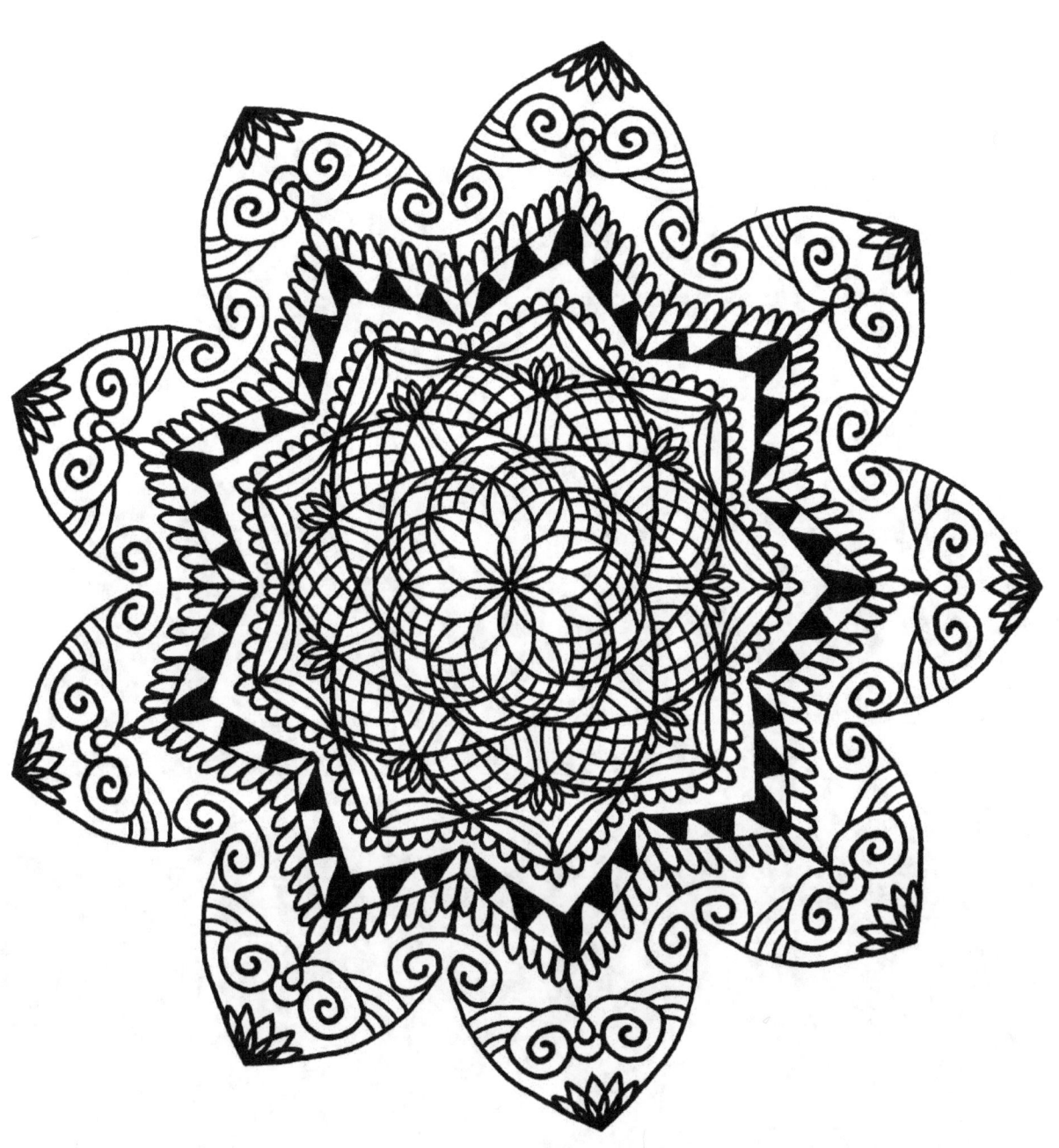

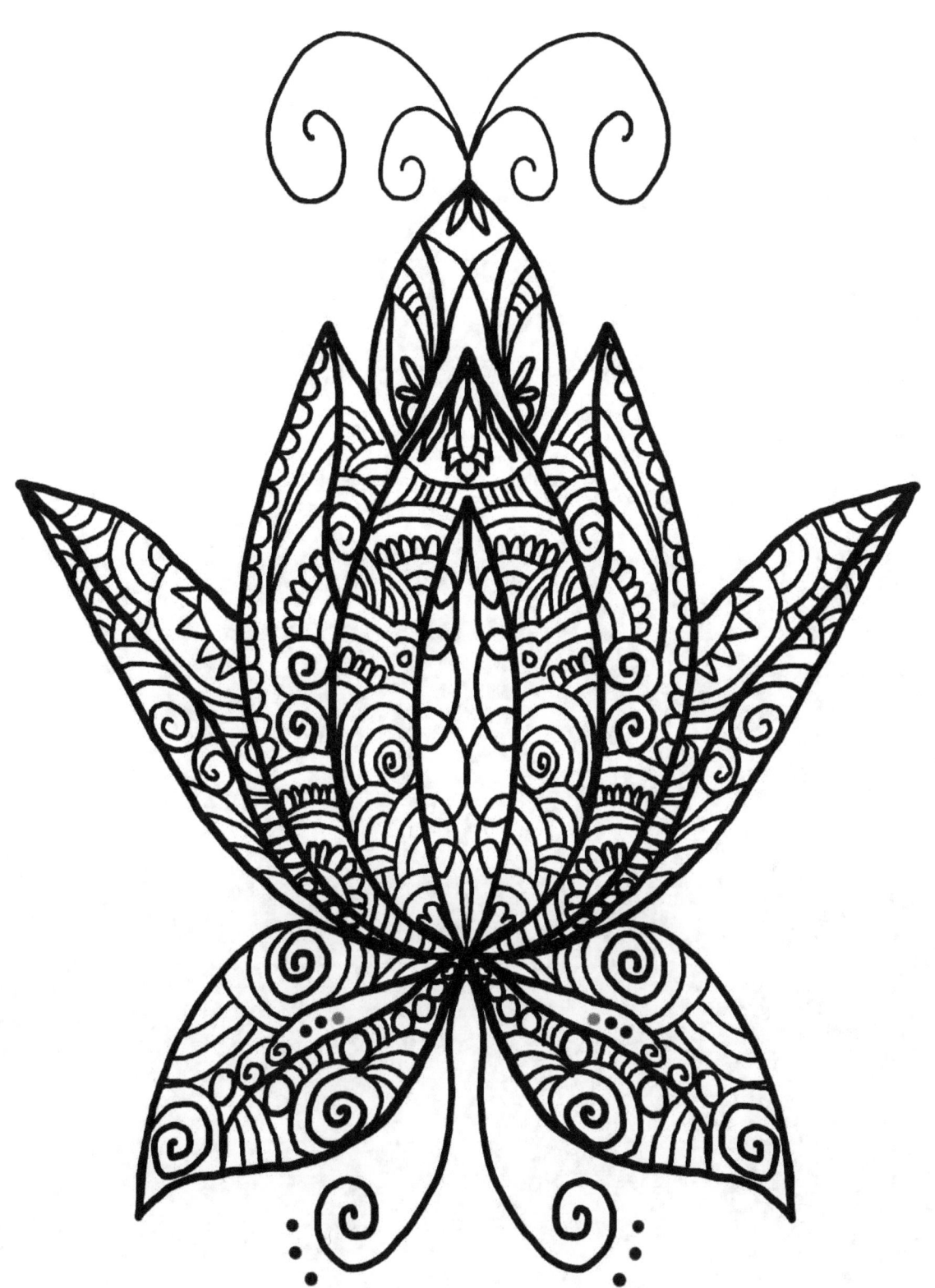

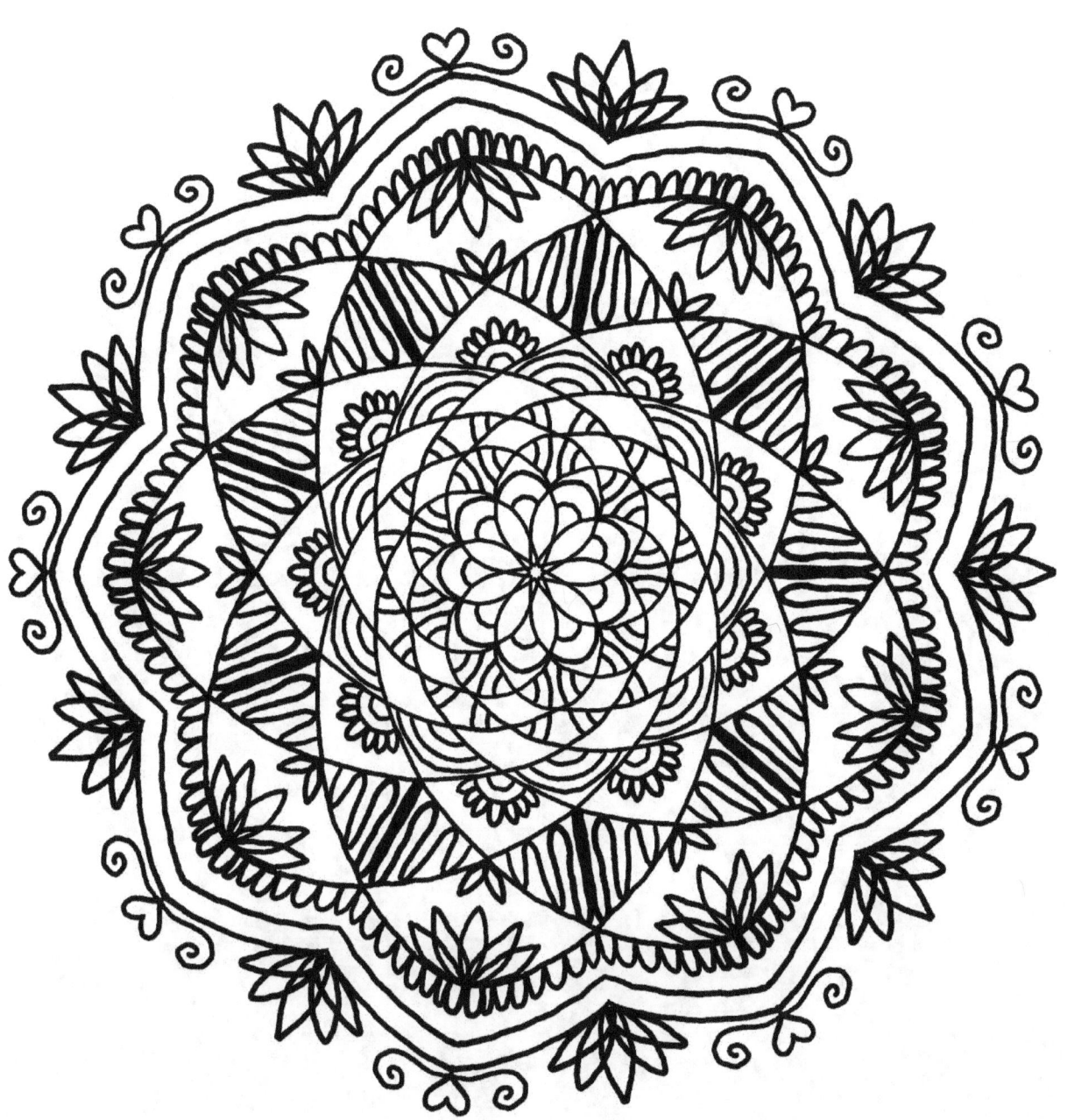

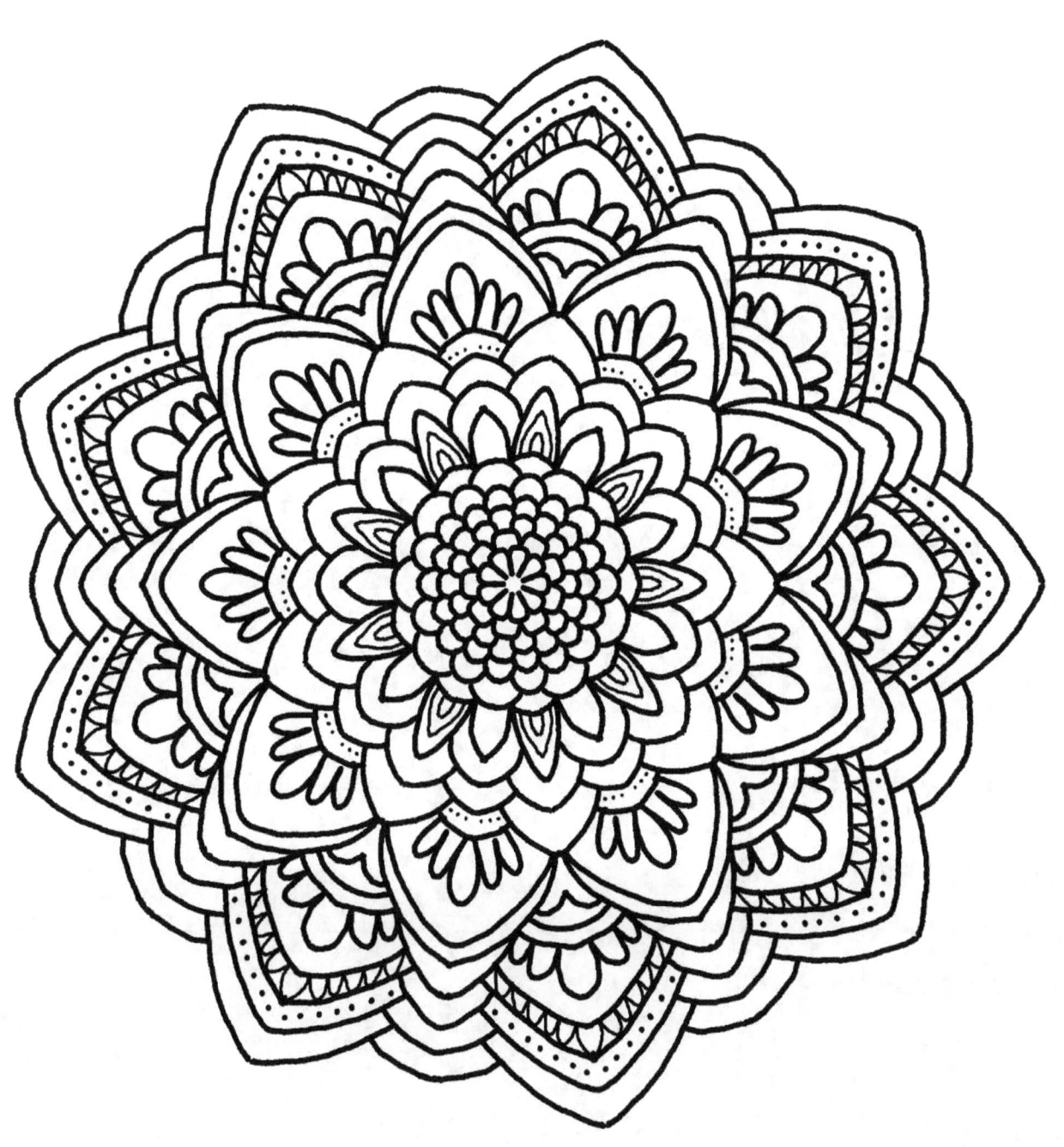

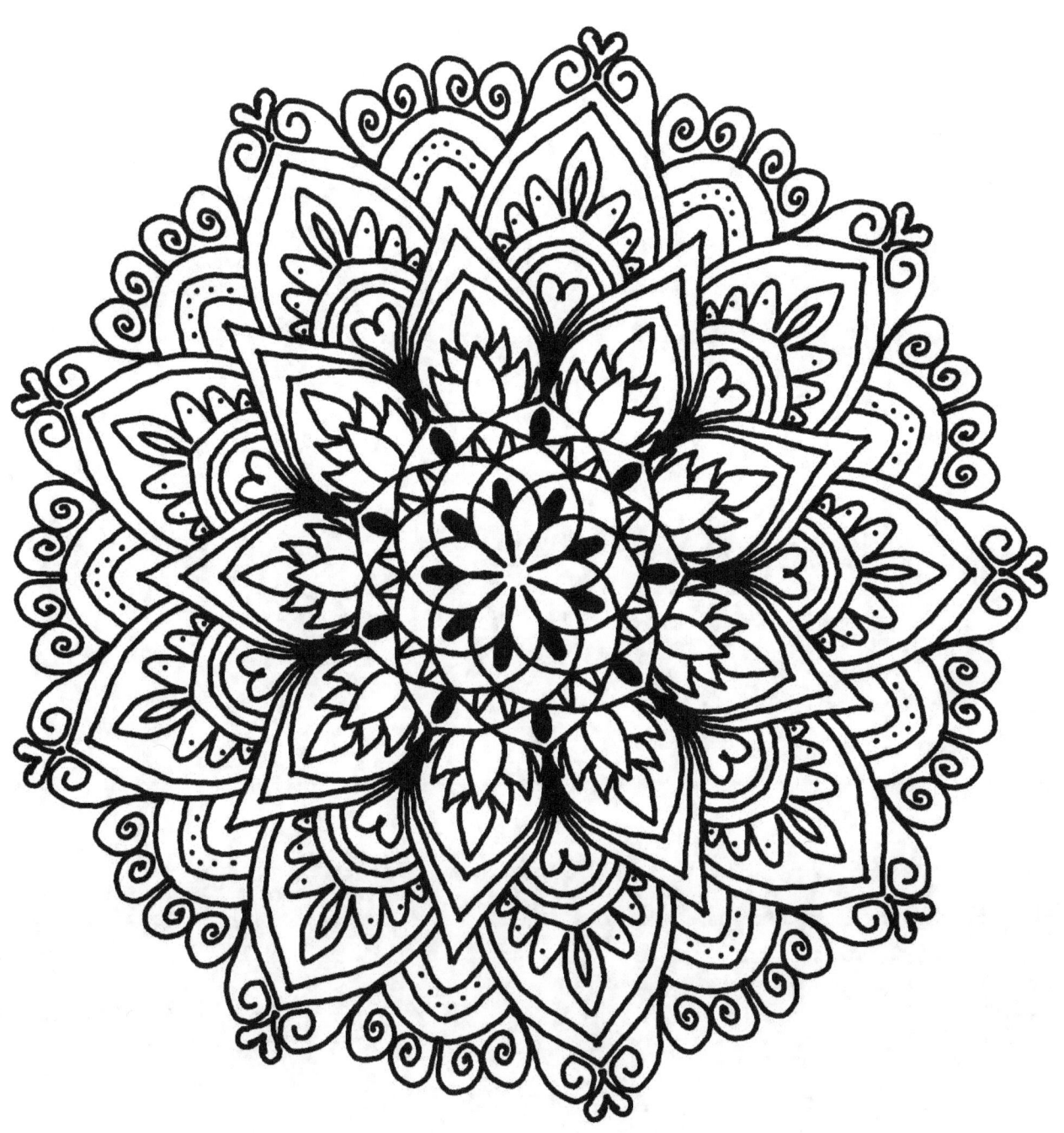

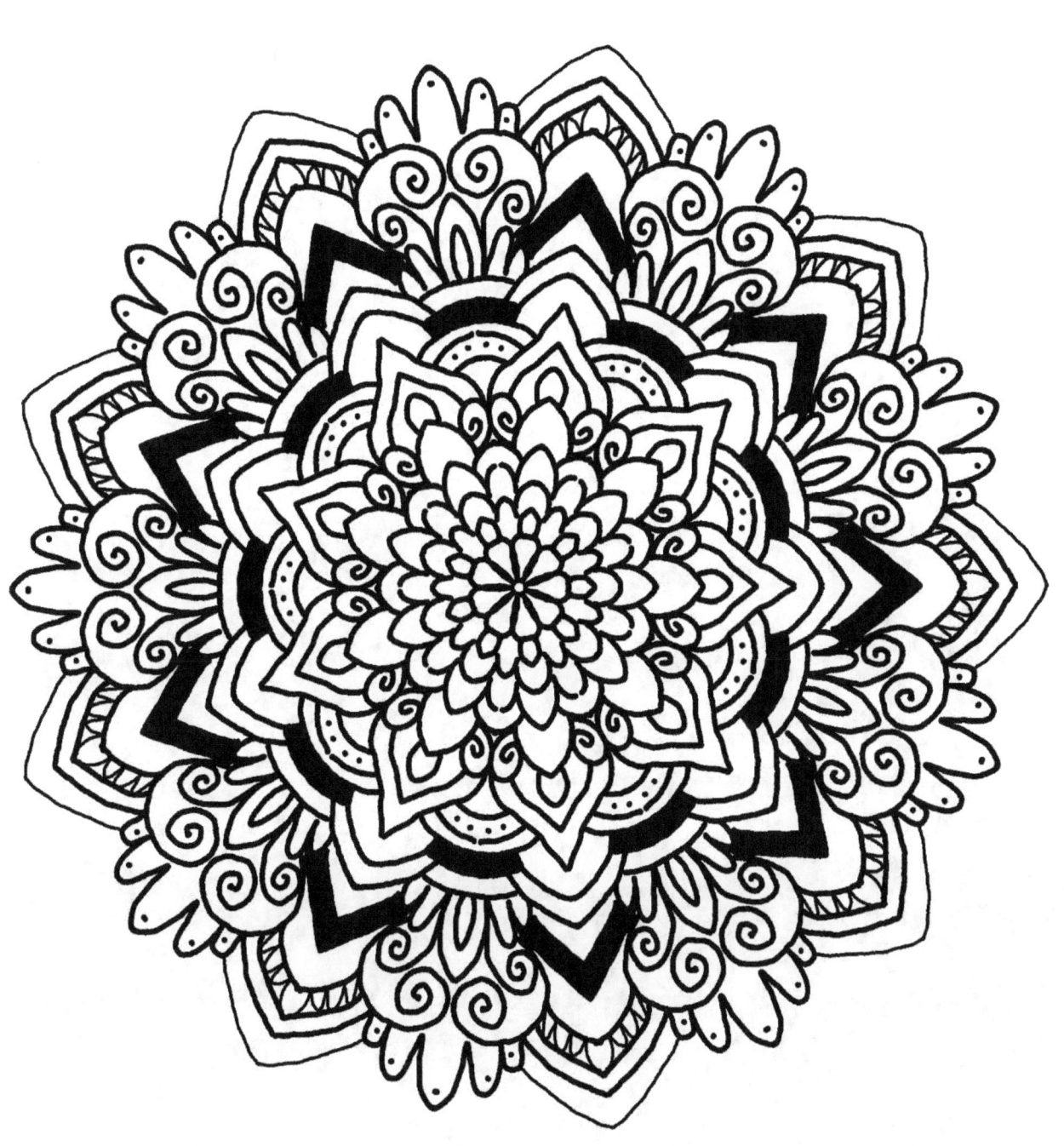

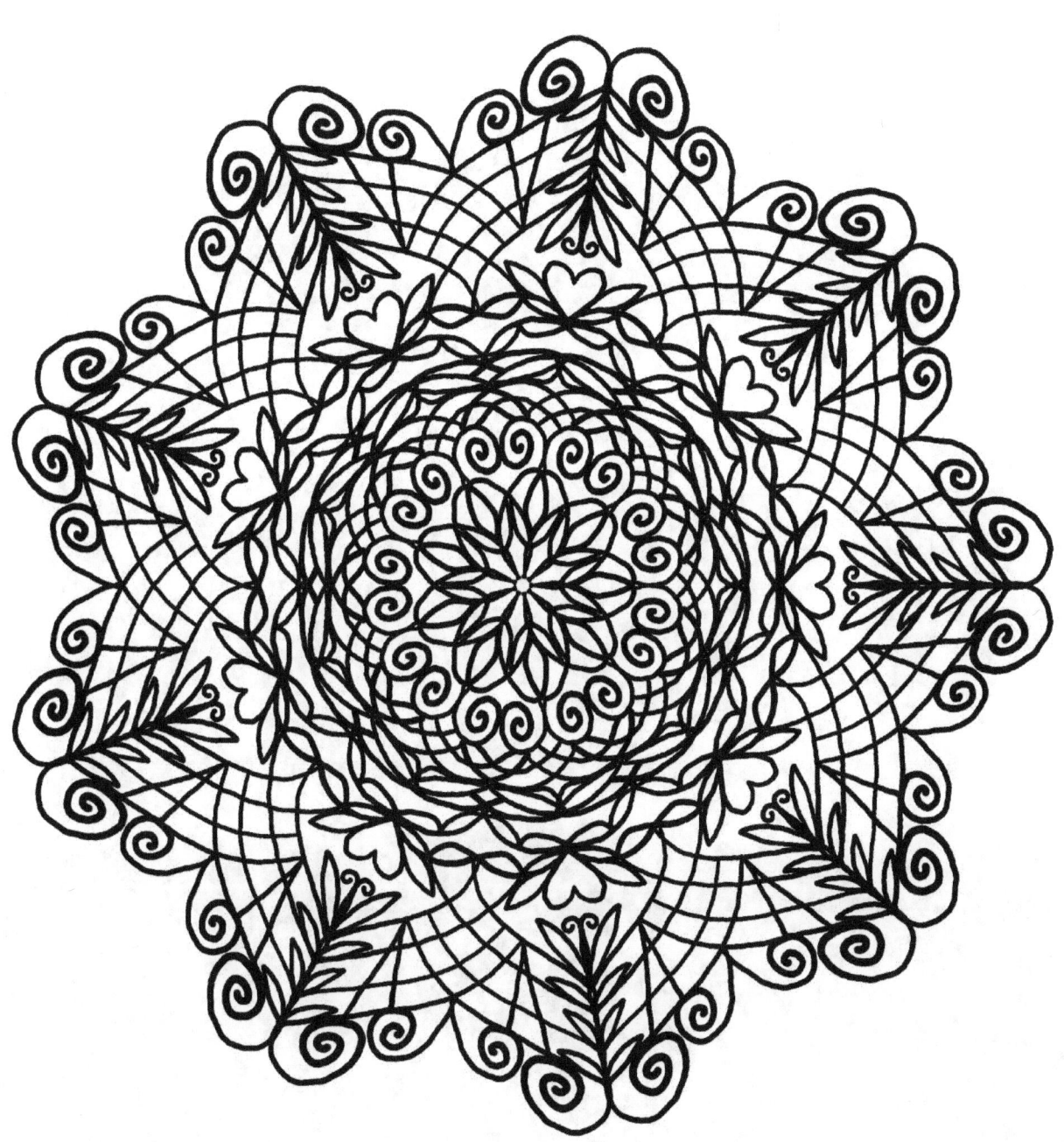

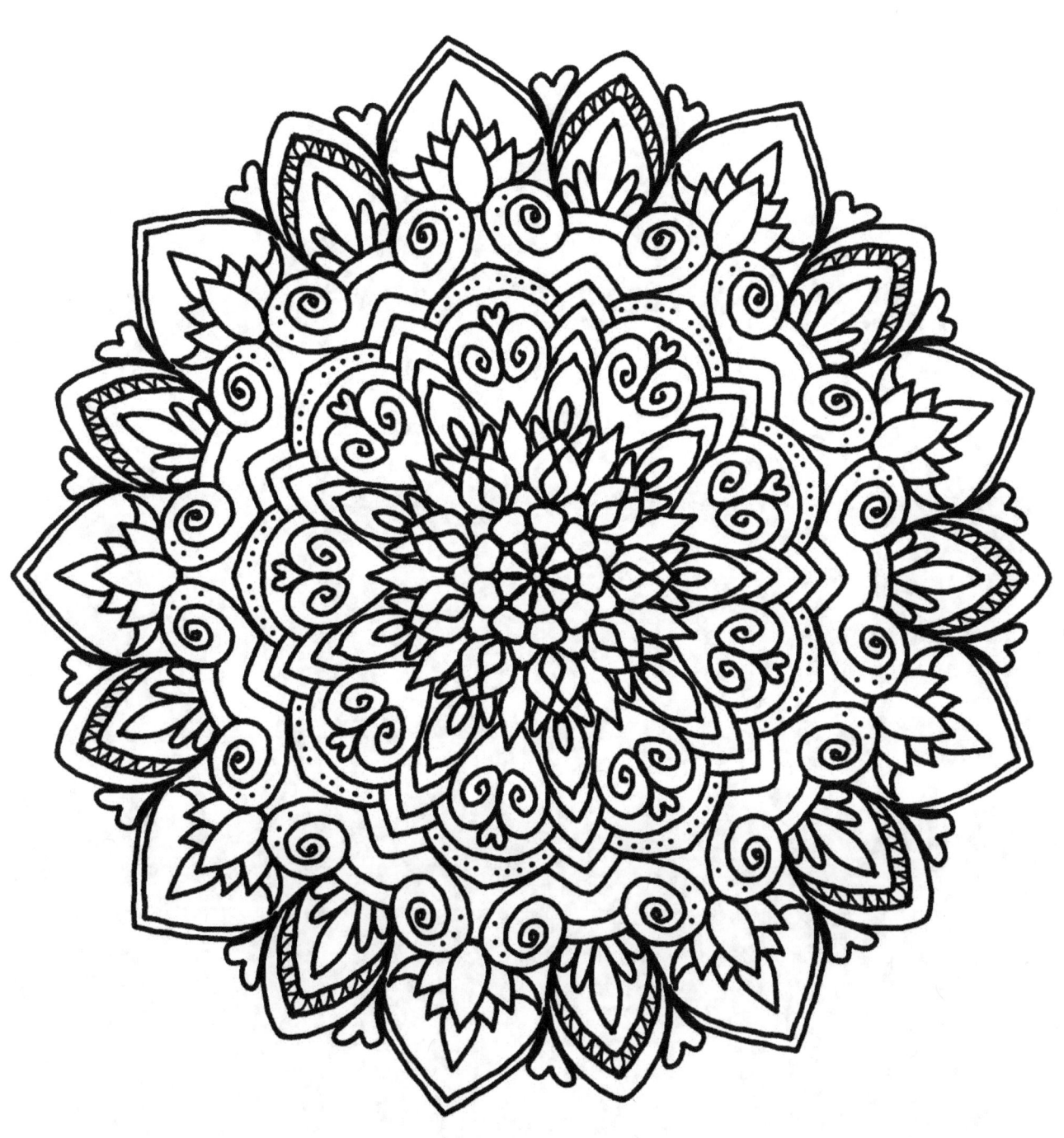

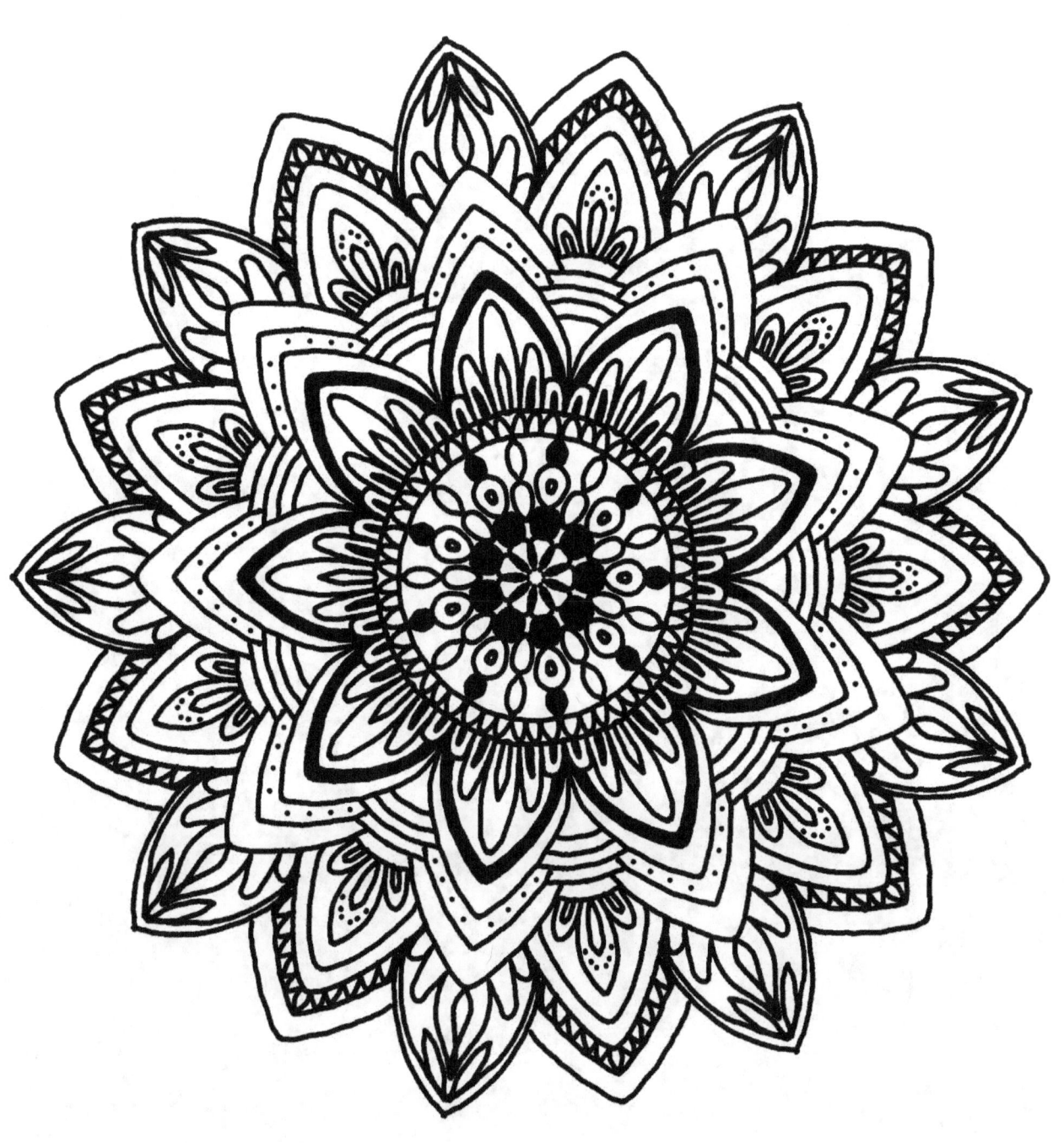

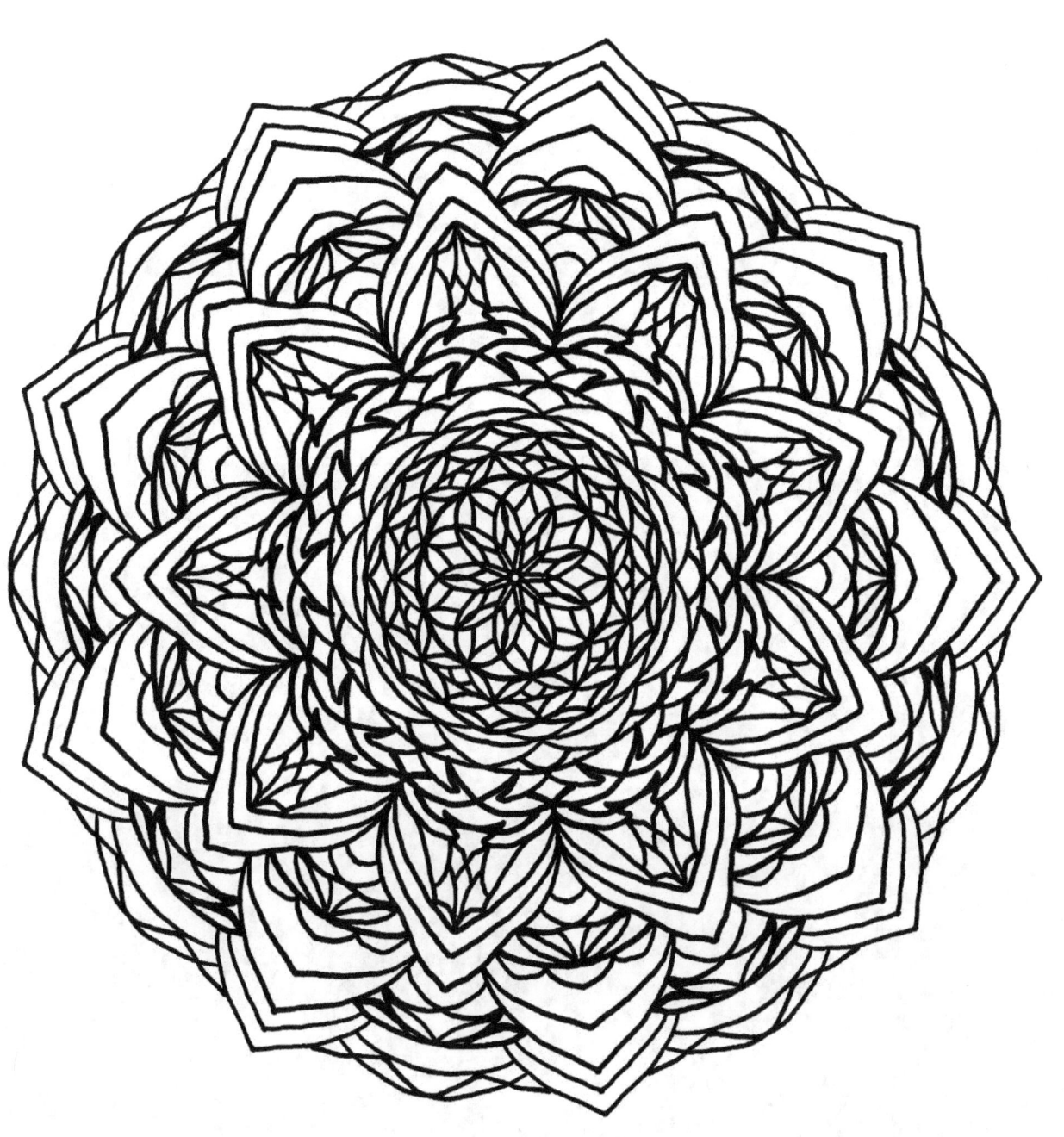

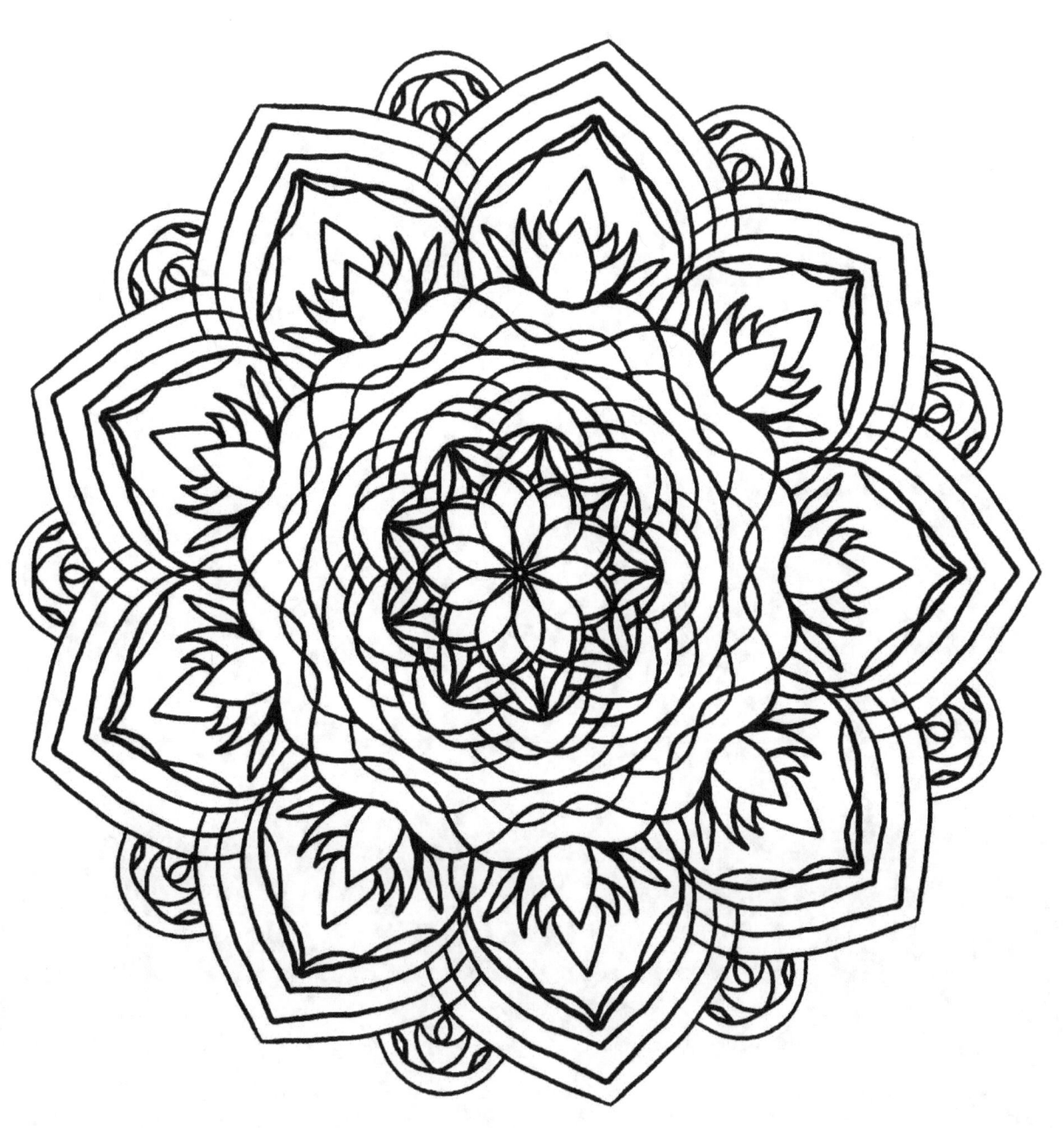

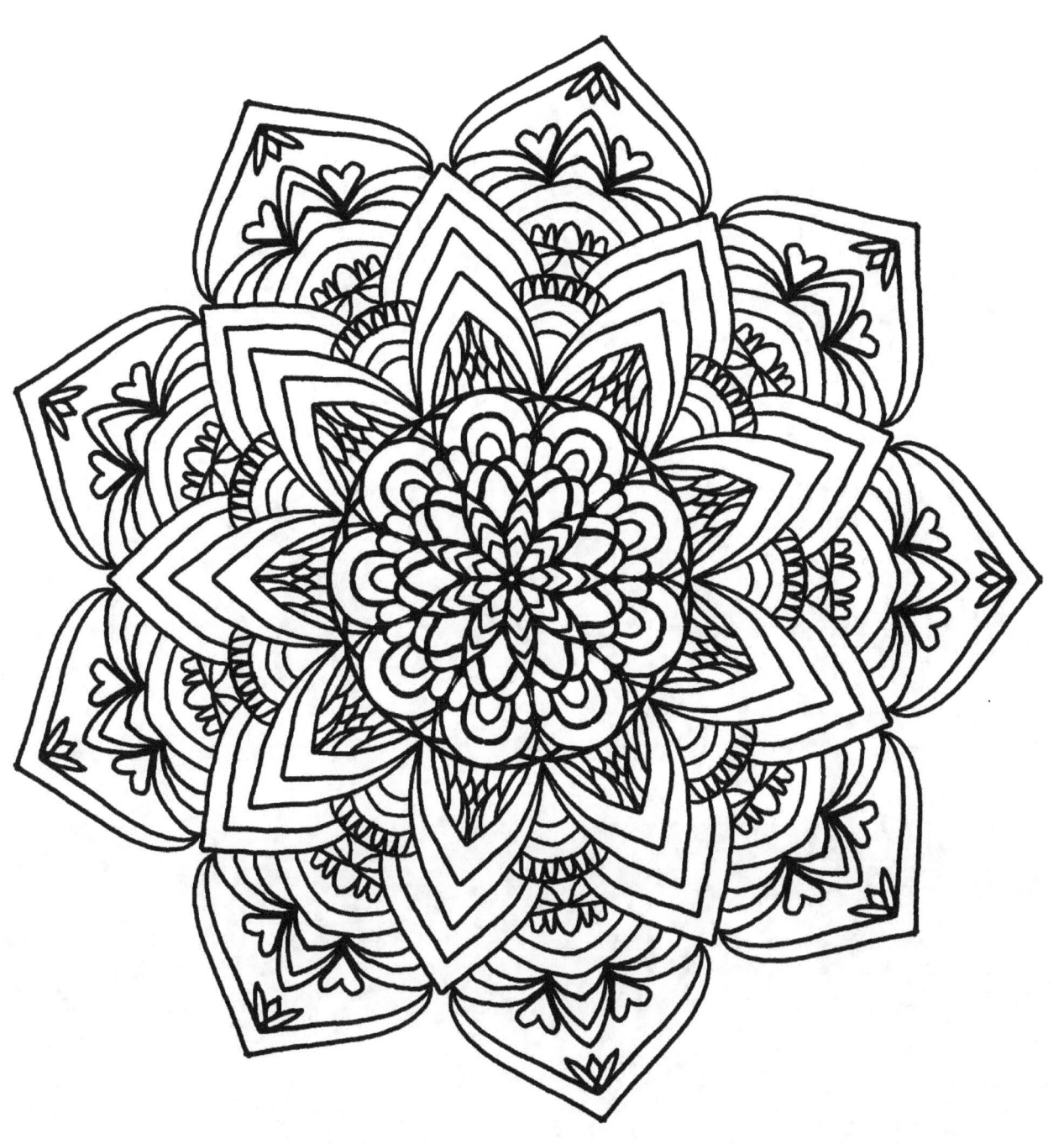

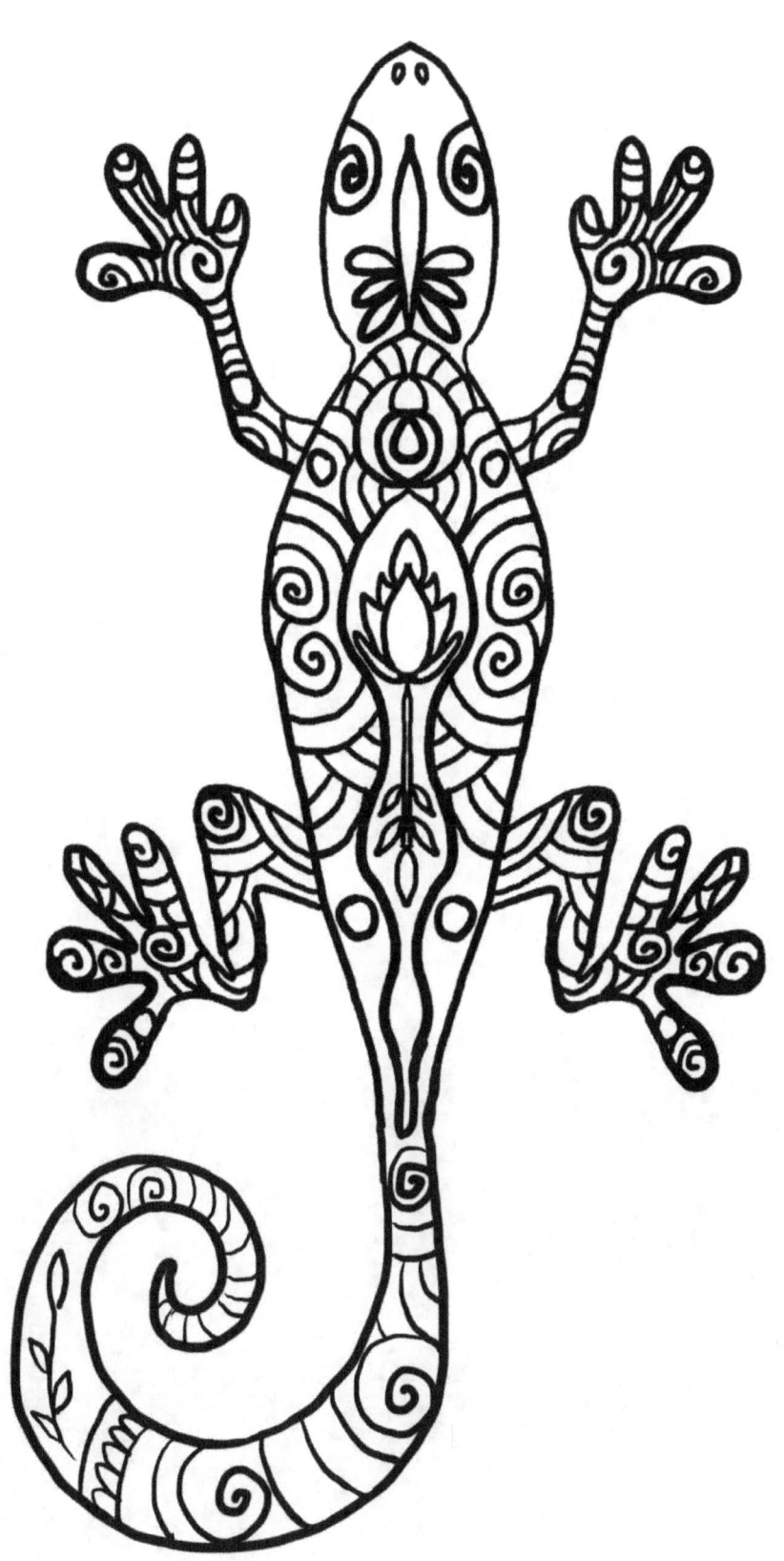

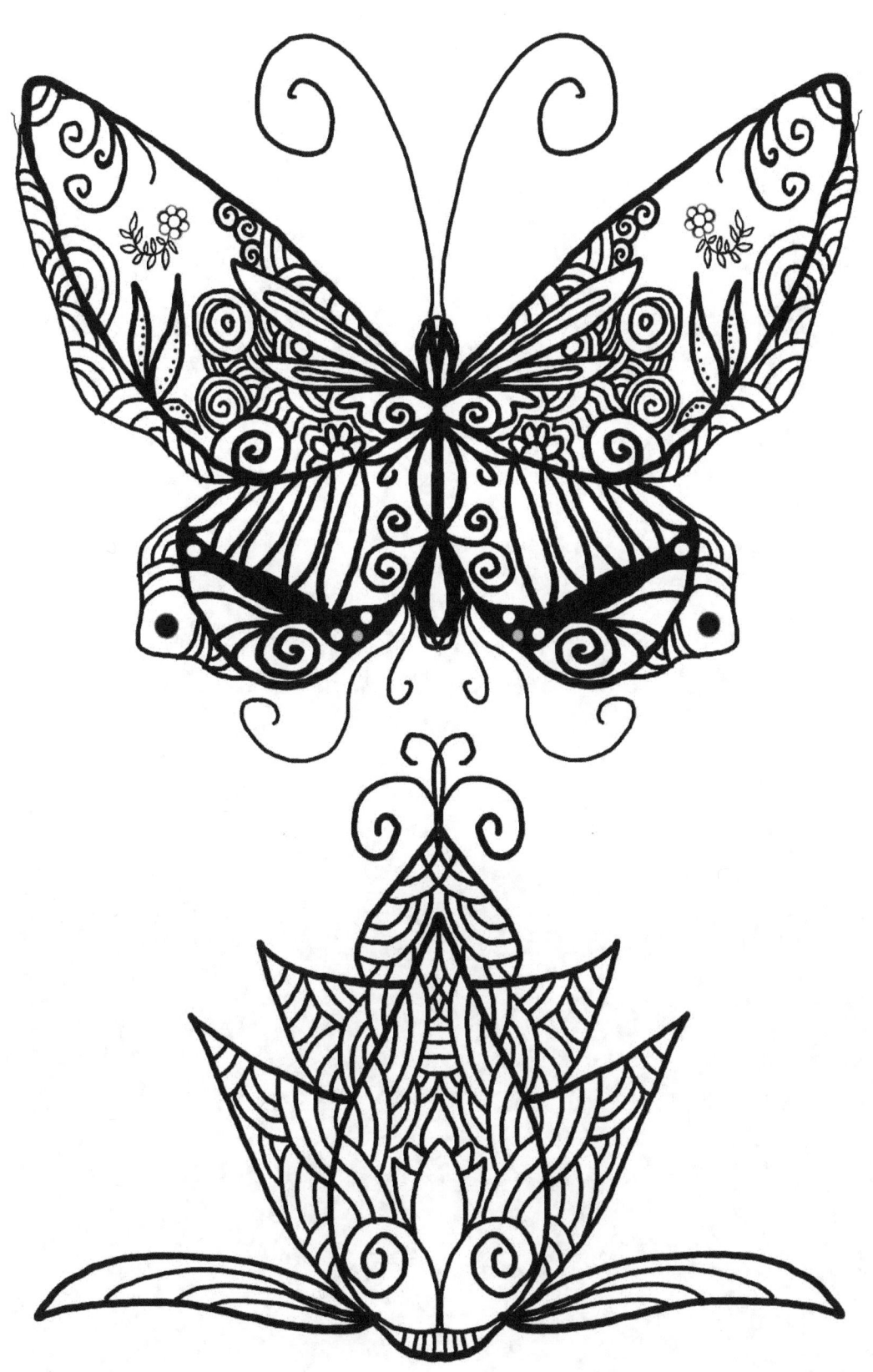

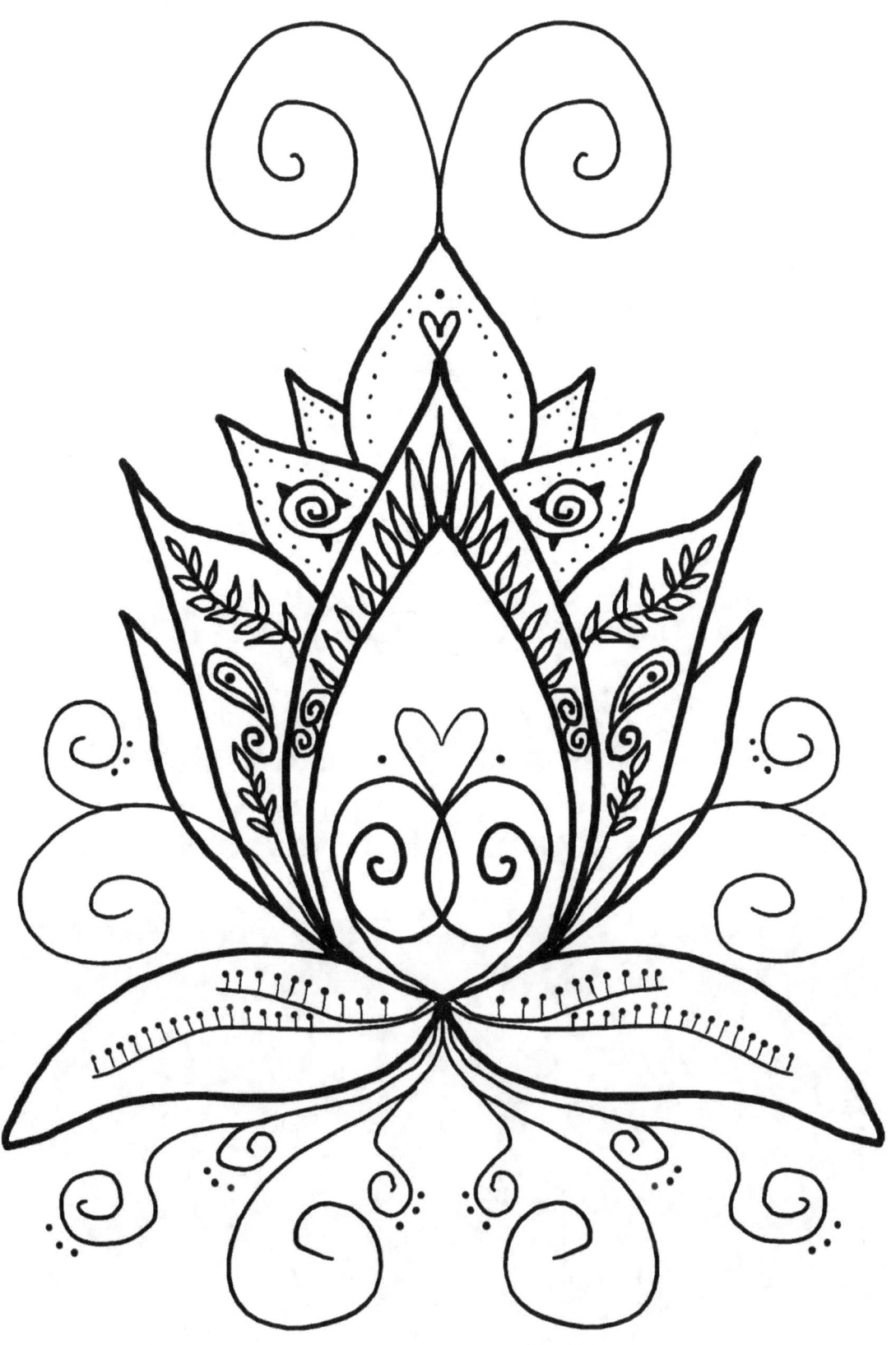

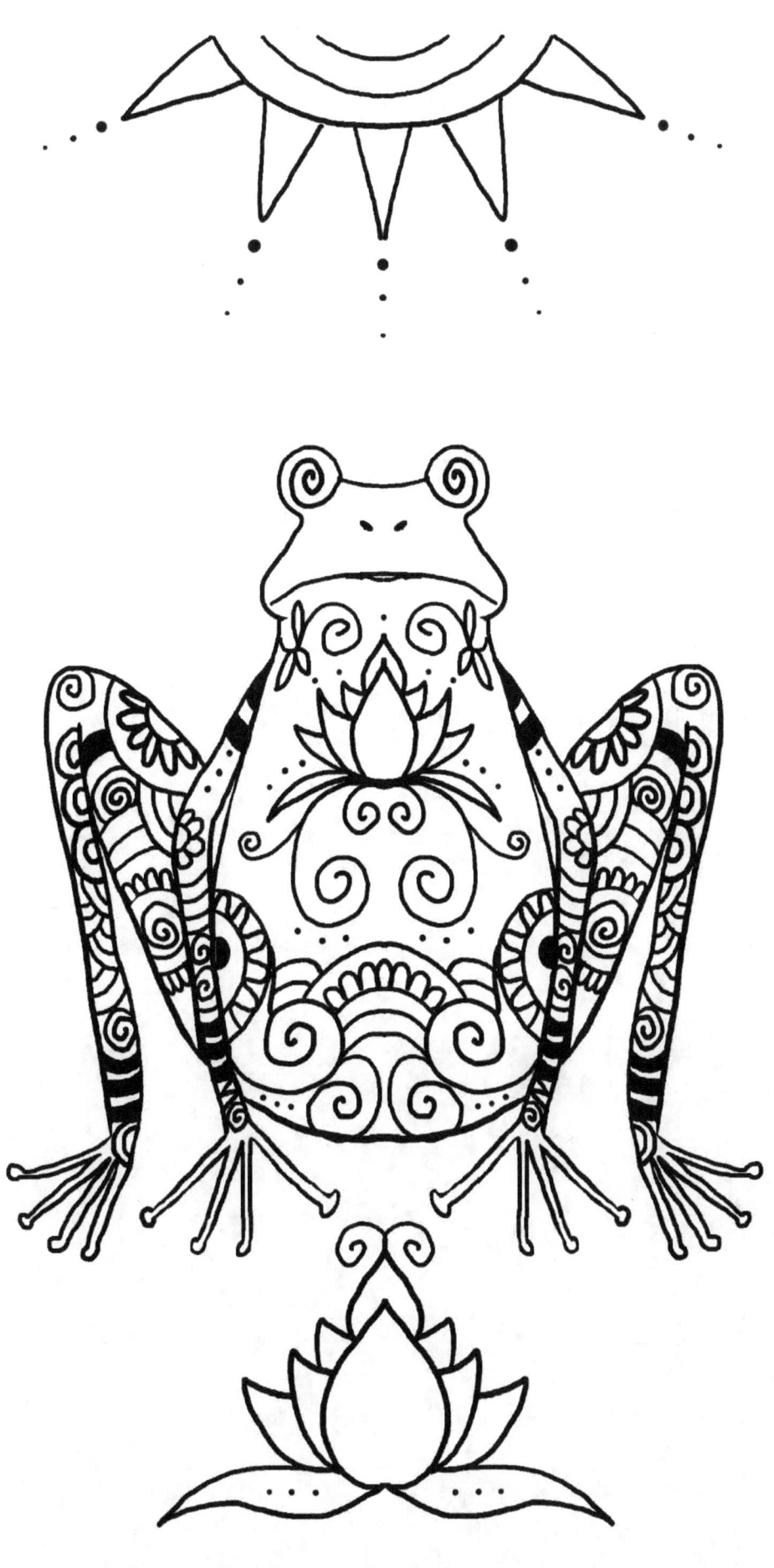

www.ingramcontent.com/pod-product-compliance
Lightning Source LLC
Chambersburg PA
CBHW062224220526
45471CB00009B/3339